MINORITIES ON CAMPUS

A Handbook for Enhancing Diversity

HOW TO ORDER ADDITIONAL COPIES

Additional copies of this *Handbook* may be purchased from the American Council on Education for $17.50 postpaid (quantity discounts available). All orders must be prepaid by money order or check (made payable to the American Council on Education) and sent to:

Publications Department
American Council on Education
One Dupont Circle
Washington, D.C. 20036

MINORITIES ON CAMPUS

A Handbook for Enhancing Diversity

edited by
Madeleine F. Green

AMERICAN COUNCIL ON EDUCATION
Washington, D.C.

ACE BOARD OF DIRECTORS

Contents

Foreword...vii

Acknowledgements xi

A Note to the Reader xv

1 Introduction 1

2 Conducting an Institutional Audit 15

3 Undergraduate Students..29

4 Graduate and Professional Students........................55

5 Faculty...81

6 Administrators 95

7 Campus Climate 113

8 Teaching, Learning, and the Curriculum 131

9 Three Institutions Making a Difference: 159
   The University of Massachusetts at Boston; Miami-Dade
   Community College; Mount St. Mary's College

Endnote

Foreword

Disturbed by the faltering pace of minority advancement in American life and by the discouraging decline of participation of minority individuals in higher education, the American Council on Education (ACE) Board of Directors convened a special meeting in February 1987 to consider how higher education could take a leadership role in rekindling the nation's commitment to the full participation of minority citizens.

One outcome of the ACE Board's deliberations was the development of the Commission on Minority Participation in Education and American Life, cosponsored by the Education Commission of the States. Former presidents Gerald R. Ford and Jimmy Carter served as honorary co-chairs of a bipartisan commission of 37 prominent Americans from government, business and the nonprofit sector. In its report, *One-Third of a Nation*, the commission delivered an urgent message to the nation "that America is moving backward—not forward—in its efforts to achieve the full participation of minority citizens in the life and prosperity of the nation."[1] The Commission called for a rededication of all segments of society to "overcoming the current inertia and removing the remaining barriers to full participation of education and in all other aspects of American life."[2]

The ACE Board also recognized that higher education's most important and productive efforts would be centered on our own campuses. In the last decade we have lost momentum in our efforts to ensure that minority groups are fully represented, welcomed, and involved on our campuses. But this cannot result in an attitude of resignation and defeat. We cannot resign ourselves to anything less than success in creating a truly pluralistic campus. The injustice is too great for a democratic nation to condone; the costs are too high for all citizens.

---

[1]*One-Third of a Nation,* a Report of the Commission on Minority Participation in Education and American Life (Washington, DC: American Council on Education & Education Commission of the States, 1988), p. 3. [2]Ibid, p. 5.

Thus, we commissioned the development of this *Handbook* to provide practical information and suggestions to assist institutions in taking action. We have diagnosed the problems; now we must renew our commitment, intensify our efforts, and lead the way for other institutions in society.

The *Handbook* captures and distills the strategies that have worked. Certainly, every campus is different, and there is no formula for success. But three important principles should guide all our efforts:

The first turns on *leadership*. Leadership, from the board of trustees and the president, is essential to deep and lasting change on campus. Without their symbolic and practical support, little enduring progress will occur. I urge my fellow presidents to take their leadership responsibilities seriously in establishing a vision and building a sense of shared purpose.

The second requirement for success is an *integrated approach* to change, reflecting a vision of the future. A vigorous effort to change a campus requires more than a special program initiated here, a minority staff member added there. Minority participation must be high on everyone's agenda, integral to the mission and the workings of the institution. Pluralism requires energy and purpose.

The third principle involves *institutional change*. If our nation's campuses are to become truly reflective of the pluralism of American life, then we must examine our assumptions, structures, and priorities. It is not enough to welcome minority individuals. We need to change the culture of our majority institutions so that all members of the community contribute and honor each other's differences. As it now stands, blacks, Hispanics, Asian-Americans and American Indians bear the entire burden of adapting to the majority culture on campus. On a truly pluralistic campus, the burden and the rewards are equally shared.

We must also recognize the costs of change—in time, funds, and in the discomfort that many will experience. Tension and controversy may appear on campus as change is institutionalized. The leaders of the American Council on Education believe that the short-term costs will be worth the long-term gains.

The Board of Directors of the American Council on Education is convinced that the issue of minority participation is higher education's most important priority. We can be proud of the progress we have made over 20 years. Now, the agenda before us is not simply to do more of the same, but to reconceptualize our approach. We must make it a concern that permeates our daily discussion, and not an isolated problem on a long list of other institutional problems.

We have the knowledge. What we need now is the vision and the will.

Judith S. Eaton
President, Community College of Philadelphia
Chair, American Council on Education Board of Directors

Acknowledgements

The *Handbook* reflects the work of many people. It blends many individual voices, campus perspectives, and experiences.

The guidance of the editorial committee, representing the American Council on Education Board of Directors and the Commission on Minority Concerns, was invaluable. The committee members were: John Di Biaggio, President, Michigan State University; Sister Magdalen Coughlin, President, Mount St. Mary's College; Alfredo G. de los Santos Jr., Vice Chancellor for Educational Development, Maricopa Community Colleges; and Kenneth A. Shaw, President, University of Wisconsin System Office.

Another important group of advisors, whose patient readings of the drafts were very helpful, were the members of the Commission on Leadership Development, chaired by Kala Stroup, President, Murray State University; the Commission on Women in Higher Education, chaired by Judith Ramaley, Executive Vice President, University of Kansas; and the Commission on Minority Concerns, chaired by Kenneth A. Shaw, President of the University of Wisconsin System Office.

The process of creating this *Handbook* began with a series of background papers and drafts authored by knowledgeable practitioners and scholars from campuses across the country. The Council is grateful to the following individuals for their contributions to this book:

Donald D. Babcock, Vice Chancellor for Planning, University of Massachusetts at Boston;

James E. Cronin, Professor of History, Montgomery College;

Johnnella E. Butler, Associate Professor, Department of American Ethnic Studies, University of Washington;

Alfredo G. de los Santos Jr., Vice Chancellor for Educational Development, Maricopa Community Colleges District Office;

Catalina Gomez-Mons, Administrative Assistant, Miami-Dade Community College;

William B. Harvey, Department of Educational Leadership, North Carolina State University;

Mardee S. Jenrette, Director, Teaching/Learning Project, Miami-Dade Community College;

Sister Kathleen Kelly, Dean of the Doheny Campus, Mount St. Mary's College;

Michael Nettles, Research Scientist, Educational Testing Service;

James P. Pitts, Dean of Academic Affairs, Ohio Wesleyan University;

Anne S. Pruitt, Director, Center for Teaching Excellence, Ohio State University;

Richard C. Richardson, Jr., Associate Director, National Center for Postsecondary Governance and Finance, Arizona State University;

Mary Ann D. Sagaria, Associate Professor, Department of Educational Policy and Leadership, Ohio State University;

Suzanne B. Skidmore, Assistant to the President, Miami-Dade Community College; and

Robert Terry, Senior Fellow and Director, Hubert H. Humphrey Institute of Public Affairs Reflective Leadership Program, University of Minnesota.

The ACE staff played a central role; the members of the "Leadership Group" were crucial collaborators at every point in the preparation of the *Handbook.* These individuals brought years of experience to the task: Sara E. Meléndez, Director, Office of Special Minority Initiatives; Marlene Ross, Associate Director, Center for Leadership Development; Donna Shavlik, Director, Office of Women in Higher Education; Judith G. Touchton, Deputy Director, Office of Women in Higher Education; and Reginald Wilson, Director, Office of Minority Concerns. Others who contributed to this effort were ACE staff members: Gail T. Kendall, Administrative Assistant, Office of Special Minority Initiatives; Andrew Malizio, Assistant Director, Division of Policy Analysis and Research; James J. Murray, Director, Division of Advancement, Membership, and Publications; and Education Policy Consultant Arthur Hauptman.

Research assistant Laurie Fuller began the long process of collecting information for the "Programs and Practices" section. Darrel Williams continued this task and succeeded in developing a remarkable compendium of information from across the nation.

The Council was also fortunate to have the editorial assistance of James Sevick and the services of Charles Aldrich and the staff of Kell & Co. in the design and production of the *Handbook.*

Finally, the Council thanks the many individuals who provided expert advice on various chapters and aspects of the *Handbook.* They included:

Toy Caldwell-Colbert, Assistant Vice President for Academic Affairs, Indiana State University;

Alice Grant, Professor of Communications, Florida Community College of Jacksonville;

Nancy Hoffman, Acting Associate Dean, School of Education, Harvard University;

James Lyons, President, Bowie State College;

Edmond Keller, Faculty Assistant/Academic Affairs, Office of the President, University of California, Berkeley;

Jacqueline Martin, Associate Professor of Biology, Tennessee State University–Nashville;

Mary Rowe, Special Assistant to the President, Massachussetts Institute of Technology;

Laura Tracy, Department of English, Georgetown University.

A Note to the Reader

To develop a handbook that is useful to a wide variety of readers in many different institutions is an ambitious, perhaps impossible task. The contributors to this volume, as well as the Board of Directors of the American Council on Education who commissioned it, recognized from the outset that this *Handbook* could not satisfy all its readers. Indeed, the diverse reactions to the drafts that were circulated for review provided ample indication that individuals would read this *Handbook* from different perspectives and receive it quite differently.

Some readers will find the contents of this book elementary. And indeed, many of the suggestions are not new; they will have a ring of familiarity. Institutions may very well have tried some of the strategies suggested and concluded that they did not work. This *Handbook* urges you to consider in more depth why that tactic did or did not work, and especially to consider each individual strategy in relation to the larger institutional goal. It does not suggest simply putting old wine in new bottles, but rather reconceptualizing the problem and revisiting familiar territory armed with new perspectives.

That is a difficult task, and the simplicity of the approaches suggested in this volume may be deceptive. Increasing minority participation will require tremendous effort and energy, institutional commitment, and leadership throughout the institution. It will require fighting the temptation to look for new roads to travel when we have not really charted or navigated the existing ones. "We've tried that and it didn't work" should be the beginning of the voyage, not the end.

Others will find that the *Handbook* does not go far enough, that it does not force readers to confront personal and institutionalized racism, that it does not hit hard enough at the obstacles preventing change. We have deliberately chosen to use positive assumptions, not because we are naive, but because we are pragmatic. Our point of departure is the good will and positive energy of the many individuals in higher education who *are* committed to positive change and to the creation of a truly pluralistic campus. Those are the people who will provide leadership; we think that this book will be helpful as they proceed.

Finally, a word about language. Because this area is emotionally charged and value-laden, words take on even greater importance. Words develop histories, positive and negative connotations that color the perceptions of readers and listeners. Commonly used terms, though a convenient shorthand, are sometimes inadequate to express the complexities of this issue. We recognize that the term "minority," because it aggregates very diverse groups, does a disservice to the blacks, Hispanics, American Indians, and Asian-Americans we include under that umbrella. Words that aggregate, such as "minority" can easily lead us to stereotype. Not all "minority" students are underprepared. "Hispanics" are Chicanos, Cubans, Puerto Ricans, Central and South Americans, peoples with different histories and traditions. Some, but not all, Asian-American students outperform their majority counterparts. In short, every group and subgroup is different. Where possible, this *Handbook* disaggregates the various racial and ethnic groups. But simplicity and economy of language make it difficult to do so consistently.

Other difficult words that are central to this *Handbook* are "diversity" and "pluralism." In a recent report issued by Brown University, the term "diversity" was used to connote "the mere presence of multiple ethnic and racial groups within the community," whereas "pluralism" has a much more positive and active connotation, since it "asks of the members of all groups to explore, understand, and try to appreciate one another's cultural experiences and heritage.[1] "Diversity" connotes passive coexistence; "pluralism" is a dynamic atmosphere of collaboration. For Brown University, a key goal is to move beyond "diversity" to "pluralism." These sharp distinctions are not always drawn by those speaking and writing on this issue; the authors of this *Handbook* have chosen to use the two terms interchangeably, with the meaning ascribed above to "pluralism" also applicable to "diversity."

The contributors to the *Handbook* fully recognize the importance of language and have tried to craft the book with care. But our

---

[1]*The American University and the Pluralist Ideal,* a Report of the Visiting Committee on Minority Life and Education at Brown University, and a Dissenting Opinion by Lerone Bennett, Jr., 1986, p. 5.

words will occasionally prove inadequate to the task. We hope that readers will keep their sights on the challenge and the solutions rather than on the vehicle of expression. Language has its limitations, human potential has few.

Madeleine F. Green
Editor

1

Introduction

THE ISSUE: LOST MOMENTUM

More than 20 years have passed since the enactment of the 1964 Civil Rights Act, and higher education has made real progress in opening up our nation's campuses to minority students. For example, in 1960 there were 150,000 black students in higher education; by 1975 that number had risen to approximately one million. But progress since then has slowed, and national commitment to equality and access seems to have faltered. Black enrollments have remained stagnant since 1975. This is not to say that institutions have failed to address the problem; indeed, campuses across the nation have put in place a variety of programs and policies to promote the recruitment and retention of minority students, faculty, and staff. However, these efforts have not produced sustained success. The gap between the participation rates of white students and minority students is growing, and attrition is a major problem. What, then, has gone wrong? Why haven't our efforts worked?

There are several possible answers to this question. The first relates to the importance of sustained efforts to improve primary and secondary schools. Black and Hispanic students are more likely to be poor. Heavily concentrated in inner city public schools, they frequently receive an education inferior to that of more affluent and white students. American Indian youngsters have a far lower graduation rate from high school than blacks and Hispanics. They, too, are handicapped by poor preparation. Students who come ill-prepared to college begin at a disadvantage, and may never catch up.

The national movement to improve primary and secondary schools has gained considerable momentum in the last ten years. Higher education institutions have joined this effort by working with public schools to expand the pool of prepared students; these initiatives will require time to bear fruit. A sustained and serious school reform movement may have its real payoff in 5, 10, or 20 years.

1

A second reason for the lack of progress is the piecemeal approach many institutions have taken to increasing minority participation. Isolated programs to attract and retain minority students, faculty, and staff keep the effort marginal to the central mission of the institution. Comprehensive, institution-wide policies and programs, nourished by vigorous leadership from the president and the governing board, are key to institutional change. Real progress requires that increasing diversity be an integral part of the institution's mission, its planning process, and its day-to-day activities.

Finally, there is the obvious answer that academe is simply slow to change. Creating a truly pluralistic campus requires profound change, both on a personal and organizational level. Human nature instinctively resists such change when the status quo is comfortable. The intrinsic rewards of justice for disenfranchised groups of citizens, or the necessity of adaptation to a new demographic reality may seem remote to the average faculty or board member. Some members of the academic community simply don't see the urgency of this issue for their lives, or their campuses.

THE CURRENT SITUATION

Before plunging into solutions, let us briefly examine the problem we are facing nationally. What have the trends been in enrollment and graduation of minority students? In the attainment of advanced degrees by blacks, Hispanics, American Indians? What is the magnitude of the task that lies ahead?

As the following data illustrate, the issue of minority participation is a continuum; every phase is linked to the previous and the succeeding one. Consider these facts about minority students:

- *Higher education's pool of students is increasingly made up of minority youth.* In 25 of our largest cities and metropolitan areas, half of the public school students come from minority groups. In 1985, 20 percent of the school-age population was minority; in 2020, that figure will rise to 39 percent.

- *College attendance by black students has slowed; the gap in participation between whites and blacks is growing.* Between 1967 and 1975, the percentage of black high school graduates 24 years old or younger who were enrolled in or had completed one or more years of college rose from 35 percent to 48 percent; over the same period, the corresponding rate for whites grew much more slowly from 51 to 53 percent. However, between 1975 and 1985, while the college participation rate for white youths continued to climb to 55 percent, the rate for blacks dropped to 44 percent. Recently released figures indicate that, in 1986, the rate for blacks rose to 47 percent.

■ *The rate of college attendance for Hispanic youths has declined in the last decade.* While the number of Hispanic students enrolled in college has increased significantly since 1975, the rate of attendance declined slightly between 1975 and 1985, from 51 percent to 47 percent.

■ *College attendance by American Indian students lags far behind black and Hispanic attendance.* A recent report by the Cherokee Nation found that only 55 percent of American Indians graduate from high school, and of these, only 17 percent go on to college.

■ *Minority students are concentrated in community colleges.* In the fall of 1986, over 55 percent of the Hispanics and just over 43 percent of the blacks attending college were enrolled in two-year institutions. Few of these students ever go on to attend or graduate from four-year institutions.

■ *Black and Hispanic students are far less likely than white students to complete a degree.* Among 1980 high school seniors who enrolled in college, 21 percent of the white students, compared with 10 percent of the black students and 7 percent of the Hispanic students, earned a bachelor's degree or higher degree by spring 1986.

■ *Blacks attending historically black colleges and universities (HBCUs) are more likely to complete a degree than those attending predominantly white institutions.* In 1984-85, HBCUs awarded 34 percent of baccalaureate degrees earned by blacks while enrolling 18 percent of black students.

■ *Black and Hispanic participation in graduate and professional education can best be described as miniscule in the areas of mathematics and the sciences.* Though the patterns are shifting, minority students are still heavily concentrated in education. In 1986, 462 blacks earned doctorates in education, but only 6 in mathematics and 8 in physics. Hispanics earned 188 in education, 12 in mathematics, and 15 in physics; American Indians earned 26 doctorates in education, one in mathematics and none in physics.

As subsequent chapters in this *Handbook* will show, the numbers are even more disheartening for minority faculty members and administrators. And numbers do not tell the whole story. Episodes of racially motivated violence or conflict on campus, the social and academic difficulties faced by black, Hispanic, and American Indian students, faculty, and staff indicate that there is much work to be done to create a pluralistic and welcoming educational environment for all.

The future of our nation is inextricably tied to an educated population that can contribute to the labor force and the economy, as well as to our national well-being. If one-third of the nation will be composed of minority persons by the year 2010, as the demographers predict, minority citizens must be included in the economic, political, social, and educational mainstream.

Higher education has a vital role to play, both as a force for social justice and in producing an educated and productive citizenry. Our future as a nation depends on our ability to reverse these downward trends in minority achievement in education and ensure that our campuses are as diverse as our country. We cannot afford to defer the dream of full participation by all citizens; it is not only unjust, but unwise.

WHAT IS THE HANDBOOK?

This *Handbook* is a practical guide for you, the trustees, presidents, administrators, and faculty—indeed the entire campus community. It is meant to assist you in your efforts to increase minority participation and to make our nation's campuses hospitable to minority students, faculty, and staff. It concentrates on strategies that have been used by institutions across the country, gleaning principles and common themes that have been identified by individuals and institutions with experience in enhancing the participation of minorities in all aspects of campus life.

Many colleges and universities are rising to the challenge. They have devised a number of imaginative and effective strategies to improve minority participation at all levels. They are addressing the issue on many fronts—developing new programs to recruit undergraduate and graduate students, convening task forces to study and improve the campus climate, and providing services to ensure the success of minority students. This book is a compendium of their experiences and successes.

It is important to begin the change process with an assessment of your current situation; Chapter 2 provides a schema for conducting an institutional audit. Every campus is different, and you will want to start at your own individual starting point.

The *Handbook* is organized into seven areas:

■ conducting an institutional audit;

■ undergraduate students;

■ graduate and professional students;

■ faculty;

■ administrators;

■ improving campus climate;

■ teaching, learning, and the curriculum.

With the exception of the final chapter on teaching, learning, and curriculum, the essence of each chapter is in its "Strategies" section.

"Strategies" suggests general directions and specific tactics you might consider in addressing each of the areas. Of course, not every one will be appropriate for your institution. The *Handbook* tries to provide as many different approaches as possible, and to encourage you to consider how they will best work on your campus.

Each chapter contains illustrative programs and practices, examples of actual programs. They represent both "typical" approaches—that is, similar programs exist on a number of campuses—and more unusual ones, which, if not one-of-a-kind, are not widely duplicated. The *Handbook* is not exhaustive; there are many campus stories not described here. Where evaluative data are available, the program description indicates this. Other programs are too new to have such information. Complete information can be obtained by contacting the resource person listed.

WHO SHOULD USE THE HANDBOOK?

Improving minority participation on campus requires everyone's commitment and hard work. If a campus-wide task force or committee does not exist, we suggest that you create one and use the *Handbook* to formulate its agenda and guide its work. Groups such as the following can use the *Handbook*:

■ a campus-wide task force consisting of representatives of all campus groups (students, faculty, administrators, governing board members) as well as members of the community;

■ the president's cabinet;

■ a departmental or interdepartmental committee;

- a task force dealing with a particular aspect of minority participation, such as recruiting and retaining undergraduate students;

- a committee of the board of trustees;

- any work group within an institution.

WORKING ASSUMPTIONS

Several general assumptions underlie this *Handbook.* You should discuss them and see how they do or do not apply to your institution:

- *All institutions are different.* Each has a different culture, history, and structure and has devoted varying amounts of attention to the issue of minority participation. What is the culture of your institution and how will it affect improving minority participation?

- *Institutions must change* in order to adapt to a new population of students. To date, many of our efforts have concentrated on "fixing" the minority students to enable them to blend into the culture and structures of the institution. Creating a truly diverse environment goes beyond absorbing 100 Hispanic students or hiring one black faculty member. How has change been accomplished in your institution in the past? Consider what it will take to change your institution with respect to minority participation. Try to construct a vision of what your institution would be like if it were truly a pluralistic environment, equally welcoming majority and minority students.

- *This is an emotionally charged and value-laden area.* People will have emotional as well as intellectual responses to this issue. Anger, frustration, unconscious and conscious emotions and values are frequently part of the discussion, and interactions; they must be recognized and addressed. How can you deal with these emotions constructively as you work?

- *The strategies suggested in this Handbook will benefit the entire campus community, not simply minority individuals.* For example, good recruiting practices will widen the net and increase access for all students. Similarly, a well-conducted search follows good employment practices, which result in a more comprehensive and equitable process. Active learning and student-centered teaching have been called for in national reports on education as beneficial to *all* learners. A diverse community of students, faculty, staff, and board members enriches the learning experience for all and helps prepare all members of the community for the multicultural world in which we live.

THE IMPORTANCE OF A COMPREHENSIVE APPROACH

The institutions that have been successful in improving minority participation have at least one important characteristic in common: **They have developed a comprehensive and institution-wide approach.** Too often in the past, institutions have tried a program here, a new staff person there. An institution-wide commitment to enhancing diversity and vigorous leadership from the chief executive officer and the governing board will produce more qualitatively different results than an institution undertaking sporadic and piecemeal efforts, even if they are well conceived and well executed.

This theme is restated throughout the *Handbook*, for it is central to understanding it and taking full advantage of it. Every topic in this *Handbook* is related to the others. For example, increasing the numbers and persistence of minority students is connected to the presence of minority faculty and to the existence of a hospitable campus environment. Although the topics are arbitrarily divided, each one depends on the ones before and after it.

A comprehensive approach requires institution-wide planning and coordination. Improving minority participation becomes a goal for all departments and academic units, a factor in the strategic planning process, a criterion by which individuals and units are evaluated. All involved must understand how the pieces fit together, and how their own roles and responsibilities relate to the whole.

GETTING STARTED

Often, the hardest part of any task is simply getting started. The bigger the issue to tackle, the more difficult it can be to get mobilized. Here are a few suggestions to assist you in beginning the process:

- *Get broad institutional involvement.* Increasing minority participation on your campus will require the active involvement of many individuals. As many members of the campus community as possible must be personally invested in the change agenda. Though many institutions feel "committeed" and "task-forced" to death, we recommend that you begin by forming a broadly representative task force to develop an institution-wide agenda. It should have the full support of the president and report to him or her. The committee should be chaired by a highly respected member of the campus community.

- *Assign overall administrative responsibility to one individual.* While minority participation must be on everyone's agenda, leadership and oversight must reside with one senior individual with the clout and resources to make things happen and to hold people accountable. We strongly recommend that this person report to the president. At the University of Washington, for example, there is a vice president for minority affairs, reporting to the president. Decentralization of recruiting students, hiring faculty, and other initiatives associated with increasing and improving minority participation can result in fragmentation of efforts. This fragmentation can be counteracted by having one person clearly in charge.

■ *Take stock of where you are, where you would like to be.* An institutional audit or self assessment is the first step in improving minority participation. The *institutional audit,* included as Chapter 2, provides a starting point. Begin by gathering data on minority students, faculty, administrators. Trace a historical picture to discern trends. Use the audit to decide what other data you need, to recognize the gains you have made, and to target areas for improvement. More detailed information on conducting an institutional audit is contained in that chapter.

■ *Develop a plan.* A plan serves as a blueprint for action. Unlike the master plans that languished on many institutional shelves a decade ago, a strategic plan should be grounded in external realities and modified as conditions change. The same is true of a plan to increase minority participation. While every institution will proceed differently, its plan will have the same basic elements. These elements follow.

ELEMENTS OF AN INSTITUTIONAL PLAN

• *Leadership statement.* A plan should begin with a vision of what the institution can and would like to be. This vision should be consistent with the institution's values and overall mission. A plan for minority participation cannot stand off alone, marginal to the other business of the institution.
• *Goals.* A vision is made concrete by establishing quantitative and qualitative, long-term and short-term goals.
• *Timetable.* Though timetables often end up being revised as reality intrudes on neatly designed plans, it is important to set target dates for the implementation of specific goals and to monitor your progress against these timetables.
• *Mechanisms for conflict resolution.* As you move forward, it is highly likely that conflict will emerge as a by-product of the change process. It is important to have a mechanism in place to address these conflicts, provide forums for resolution, and to prevent the escalation of conflict. Suggestions for creating these mechanisms are described in the next section.

- *Monitoring, accountability, and evaluation.* A plan is only useful if it is monitored for its effectiveness and practicality. To do so requires assignment of responsibility for particular tasks to individuals and groups, and assignment of overall responsibility to a senior person on campus.

STRATEGIES FOR SUCCESS

While strategies will vary from campus to campus, there are certain constants that undergird successful efforts.

- *Leadership from the top.* It is important that governing boards and chief executive officers be fully committed to the goal of enhancing minority participation and that this commitment be demonstrated in word and deed. Statements of purpose and commitment issued by the board and/or president are important beginnings, both symbolically and actually. Diversity on the board, on the presidents' staff, the celebration of diversity in all aspects of campus life, and the clear willingness to allocate resources to achieve equity are but a few concrete demonstrations of leadership.

- *Leadership from the ranks.* While the commitment of the board and president are important, they cannot accomplish real change without support and leadership throughout the institution. For example, any individual hiring a new staff member can actively recruit minority candidates by contacting colleagues at other institutions for suggestions rather than simply relying on responses to advertisements. Similarly, department chairs play a key role in developing strategies to recruit minority graduate students through networks in their own discipline. Faculty involvement in all phases of institutional planning and implementation is crucial. In short, institutional change is the sum of many individual actions.

- *Involvement of minority persons.* While this sounds obvious, it is a crucial point. The planning effort will be sound or successful only with the input of affected groups and with their participation in the formulation of the agenda and potential solutions.

- *Support of minority networks.* Networks of minority students, faculty, and staff are key to providing them with information and support. Institutional leaders can support these networks by providing resources and recognition.

- *Mentoring for students, faculty, and staff.* An advisor and an advocate will help all individuals grow personally and professionally as well as learn the system. Mentoring programs are especially useful to minority individuals to develop relationships with both majority and minority colleagues and to be sure that they have advisors and advocates.

■ *Allocation of sufficient resources.* Some of the strategies recommended in this *Handbook* and others that you will develop will cost money. Finding the money to achieve your objectives may mean that something else is *not* done. Discussions and decisions regarding allocation of resources to minority concerns must be incorporated into the ongoing institutional planning process.

■ *Provision of incentives.* People need encouragement and rewards to change. Incentives may be as abstract as encouragement and public recognition of accomplishments. Or, they may be as concrete as awarding extra faculty positions, extra departmental resources, or including criteria for performance appraisals that are related to the goals of improving minority participation. If necessary, sanctions can be applied to those individuals or units that are uncooperative.

■ *Explicit and result-oriented efforts.* It is important that the main goals be translated at every stage into short-term goals that are easily identified and understood. Some efforts will be easily quantifiable. For example, you might decide to increase new minority freshmen five percent over two years or hire one minority faculty member during that time period. Other, more qualitative changes will need to be broken down into a series of defined steps. For example, improving campus climate may include an institutional audit, identification of problem areas, and suggested strategies for each area, followed by reassessment. Specific outcomes, quantitative and/or qualitative, should be identified for all targets of institutional change. Progress must be regularly assessed against the yardstick of your desired outcomes. Appropriate schedules for meeting these targets should be established.

■ *A good complaint system.* A formal grievance procedure to handle discrimination or harassment complaints is essential. But many people prefer informal dispute resolution for most (but not all) problems. Most people would rather deal with the problem and arrive at a satisfying solution than "win the case." The informal complaint system or process will be structured differently on different campuses. For example, there may be a specially designated ombudsperson (there are two at the Massachussetts Institute of Technology), or a task force charged with the responsibility. One hopes that most disputes will be resolved in the work group. Whatever the structure, the mechanisms should be able to do the following:

- Deal with feelings of anger, frustration, or fear experienced by the parties involved.
- Give and receive data on a one-to-one basis.
- Counsel clients to explore options; help people make responsible choices; help them deal with problems directly if they choose to do so.
- Provide shuttle diplomacy by a third party or have the third party bring together the people with the problem so that they can reach their own settlement.
- Perform fact finding, informally or formally. Results may be used or reports made, either with or without recommendations from the fact finder to the decision maker.
- Decide disputes.
- Make recommendations for systems change.

(Adapted from Mary Rowe, "Skills Needed by a Complaint Handler and Functions Required in a Good Complaint System," Massachussetts Institute of Technology, 1988).

- *Manageable goals.* Most would agree that change in the academy is often difficult and slow. Thus, it is helpful to think big, but start small, setting goals that can be reasonably attained. A steady stream of incremental changes will have an enduring impact. It is important to monitor progress toward the goals and to keep to your schedule. Periodic evaluation may warrant adjustment and modification of your goals.

- *Periodic reporting to the president and governing board.*

ATTEMPTING A COMPREHENSIVE APPROACH: THE UNIVERSITY OF WISCONSIN SYSTEM PLAN

In April 1988, the University of Wisconsin System Board of Regents approved a plan presented by President Kenneth A. Shaw for a comprehensive system-wide strategy to increase diversity among the institutions of the University of Wisconsin (UW) System. President Shaw involved the entire university community in developing a *Design for Diversity*; the plan also involves individuals throughout the university in the implementation of the various tasks.

The goals of the plan are far-reaching, including improved recruit-ment and retention of minority students, faculty, and staff; removal of financial barriers to college attendance; the establishment of ef-fective partnerships with schools, businesses, and government; and educating all students for an increasingly multicultural society. Each of these general goals is translated into specific objectives; costs and timetables for implementation are also specified. For ex-ample, the plan indicates a goal of increasing the number of new minority freshmen and transfer students by 50 percent from cur-rent levels by fall 1993 and doubling the current number by 1998.

Mechanisms to ensure accountability are also presented in the plan. At the end of the report, a summary of 29 specific responsibilities, the timetable, and the individual or group accountable for imple-mentation leave no doubt as to how this ambitious plan will be carried out. A special assistant to the president will oversee imple-mentation. Finally, and perhaps most important, each of the chancellors of the UW institutions is charged with the responsibili-ty of developing a comprehensive institutional plan to implement the system master plan.

At the institutional level, the *Madison Plan*, issued in February 1988 by UW-Madison Chancellor Donna Shalala, presents a blue-print for change. It covers the same general areas as the system plan, specifying programs and actions that faculty, administrators and staff will undertake. For example, to achieve the general goal of helping students achieve a pluralistic perspective, an ethnic stud-ies credit requirement will be put in place by the fall of 1989, and a committee of the faculty senate is charged with developing rec-ommendations to the university-wide Academic Planning Council. The action plan is specific to the UW-Madison campus, and the accountability rests with specific individuals or groups on the cam-pus. Like the system plan, the *Madison Plan* concludes with a sum-mary that specifies tasks, individuals, and timetables.

Note: *The University of Wisconsin System Plan incorporates many of the features of a comprehensive approach described in this chap-ter. Since it has only been recently developed, outcome data are not yet available.*

CONCLUSION

Greater minority participation will improve the quality of campus life for all. All students will benefit as the curriculum is broadened and different perspectives are introduced and as the teaching and learning processes are adapted to meet different learning styles. The presence of minority faculty can serve to inspire students to achieve as well as to introduce faculty colleagues to new perspectives.

Many institutions have begun the effort to make their campuses truly reflective of the rich diversity of this country. Three such institutions are profiled in the concluding chapter. Surprisingly, we know a great deal about what works.

No handbook has all the answers; there is no sure-fire recipe for success. But this volume presents the distilled experience of many colleges and universities that have tried and achieved some success.

Your campus can succeed, too.

2

Conducting an Institutional Audit

A sustained effort to improve minority participation begins with an assessment of the history and current status of your institution. This audit is not an end in itself, of course. It forms the basis for developing a comprehensive plan to increase minority participation. Your current situation is most meaningful when considered in relation to past achievements and failures. Establishing these benchmarks will help you identify new goals and assess your progress toward them.

This chapter provides suggestions for collecting information that will form the basis of an institutional audit. (Sample worksheets to use in data gathering are included at the end of this section.) It also provides a series of questions on institutional policies and practices that will guide you in assessing the usefulness of the structures and policies now in place. Both the database and the checklists are designed to get you started, providing information on the institution as a whole, then narrowing the scope to the school or college and department level. As your task force proceeds, you will also want to use the checklists at the end of each chapter. A simple procedure is to have each appropriate department or unit conduct a self-assessment using the checklists from the various chapters and then share their results with the task force.

DEVELOPING THE DATABASE

We have already suggested that an institution-wide commitment to improving minority participation begins with the appointment of a task force or committee charged with the responsibility of gathering information, making recommendations, and monitoring progress. The first task of the committee should be to develop a profile of minority participation in all aspects of campus life. Most of this information has already been collected for federal or internal reporting. Thus, the committee will need to put the data from many different parts of the institution together, to

15

interpret it, and to use those findings as a basis for future action.

Creating an Institutional Profile

An overall profile of minorities in the institution forms the essential groundwork. Three variables are suggested:

1. Time frame. Working back from the current year, decide on the time frame of your profile. For example, you might decide to take a snapshot of the institution at three points in time: the current year, five years ago, and ten years ago. The sample worksheets use this ten-year time frame. Alternatively, you could take a similar count eight or ten years ago, and then track the last five years year by year.

2. Target groups. Develop a list of the groups you wish to profile, for example, governing board, administrators, faculty, professional staff, hourly employees. Decisions must be made at each step on how precisely to aggregate or disaggregate a particular group. For example, faculty can be counted as one group, or looked at in more detail as full-time, part-time, tenured, non-tenured. The more specificity you have, the more accurate your assessment will be.

3. Ethnic and racial groups. A simple way to proceed is to use the Equal Employment Opportunity (EEO) reporting categories: white (non-Hispanic), black (non-Hispanic), Hispanic, Asian, American Indian, Pacific Islanders. Each category should be reported by sex. You may want to disaggregate ethnic groups to pinpoint those which are underrepresented. For example, Hispanics of Mexican, Puerto Rican, or Cuban origin might be separately counted, or Asians listed as Chinese, Japanese, Vietnamese, Korean, and so forth.

Sample worksheets A1, A2, and A3 give examples of different worksheets that can be created to gather data on the institutional level. Consider developing worksheets to profile the following groups:

- Governing board
- Faculty
- Senior administrators
- Mid-level administrators
- Department chairs and unit heads
- Professional staff

- Support staff
- Undergraduate students

For each worksheet, you will need to select the relevant descriptive categories. For example, for undergraduate students, the categories (full-time and part-time students, resident and commuter, adult and traditional college-age) may not be relevant to your particular student body.

School and Unit Profiles

The second level of the data profile deals with schools, departments, institutes, and other components of the institution. Examples of units to provide data are the various schools and colleges' different administrative units (admissions, development, athletics, the counseling center). These data will pinpoint where progress has been made within the institution, as well as areas that require additional effort.

The profile of each school or unit should be developed by that group for the institutional task force. Like the institutional profile, the school or unit database would also contain at least the following three variables: time frame, target groups, ethnic and racial groups. The time frame should be consistent with the one used in the institutional profile, as should the ethnic and racial reporting categories. To the extent possible, the display of information on the target groups within each unit or school should also be consistent. For example, the various schools would provide information on all the departments, reporting on undergraduate and graduate enrollments, majors, full-time and part-time faculty, professional and support staff.

Sample worksheets B1 and B2 follow the format and principles as the institutional worksheets. They are, in effect, a disaggregation of the information presented in the institutional worksheets. The same categories listed above (e.g., undergraduate students, graduate students, faculty) can be used to profile a college.

Finally, the process should also gather information on the departmental level, profiling graduate and undergraduate students, faculty, majors, and other components you deem important. Sample Worksheet C repeats the format for a department.

Since the same worksheet format can be used for the institutional, school, and department levels, you may want to develop a master worksheet for distribution to all individuals and groups completing the worksheets; each one can then fill the appropriate blanks.

Creating a Community or State Profile

If your institution draws students from a specific community, state, or region, it is important to know the demographic composition of the area. It is useful to track the population from which you are drawing your students, using the same categories of race/ethnicity and sex, and the same years as you use in the institutional profile. You will define the geographic area that you consider important, depending on your type of institution, and the counties, states, or region from which you draw. A profile of the following populations will be a helpful basis for knowing how well you are doing in terms of the available pool:

- General population of surrounding counties, states, or region
- High school graduates of surrounding communities, states, or region

This exercise will be most useful to institutions that draw students from a clearly defined geographical area. You may be able to develop a similar profile of local college graduates for those graduate programs that recruit students in a particular state or region. Finally, since individuals for many administrative and most classified positions are recruited locally, you will want to know the composition of the available pool for these jobs.

POLICY ISSUES

While a quantitative profile is an essential first step, numbers do not tell the entire story. In assessing your progress in improving minority participation and in charting your course for the future, it is important to know what level of commitment has been made to this issue by the board, the administration, and every group on campus. A sustained and institution-wide commitment to pluralism involves developing policies and procedures, implementing them, and constantly monitoring their success. The following checklists are intended to provide a starting point for various groups in the institution to assess their policies and practices, to modify them and to develop new ones that will address the issue of minority participation.

Checklist of Institutional Policies

Each checklist enumerates certain policies, procedures or programs that institutions might have in place. Respondents may be the institutional task force charged with the issue of minority participation, groups or individuals such as the governing board, president, senior administrators, deans, department chairs, the faculty senate, student groups, institutional research and planning staff. Each of the questions should be considered in light of the considerations outlined below:

- If the answer to the question on the checklist is *yes*, is the strategy or policy effective? How do you assess how well it is working? Do you have outcome data?
- If the answer is *no*, would such an approach be important to your institution to improve minority participation? How high a priority would you place on developing such a policy or strategy?

  1. Is increasing minority participation an institutional priority? Has the governing board approved a policy designed to increase minority participation? Does it include specific goals? Has it been presented to the entire campus community?

  2. Have the various colleges, schools, units, and departments developed policies and plans to improve minority participation? Are the unit plans centrally monitored and coordinated? Do they regularly assess and report their progress to the president and board?

  3. Are there regular reviews of institutional progress by the president and board?

  4. Are there individuals in various units or schools designated to identify and document problem areas and to recommend a course of action?

  5. Are there routine collections of data on minority participation and dissemination of that data to the campus community?

  6. Are admissions criteria and practices reviewed periodically to determine if they are consonant with increasing minority enrollments?

7. Are dormitory and campus life activities reviewed periodically to determine if they are consonant with the institutional effort to provide a climate that respects a pluralistic culture?

8. Does the allocation of resources to programs to improve minority participation reflect the governing board policies on this issue? Are there sufficient institutional dollars as opposed to "soft money" to support the integrity and continuity of such programs? Which programs are scheduled to be absorbed into the regular practices and general fund budget of the institution?

Checklist of Institutional Procedures

1. Is there an affirmative action officer or person charged with the responsibility of monitoring employment policies and procedures and grievances? Does that person hold orientation sessions with search committees? have the authority to do his or her job effectively? report to the president?

2. Are there informal mechanisms to hear complaints and resolve disputes? Is there a grievance procedure related to racial and ethnic equity which is widely publicized on campus? Is input sought on the effectiveness of the grievance procedure? If so, from whom?

3. Is there a person designated to monitor the campus climate with respect to racial tolerance?

4. Are there clear policies on sexual and racial harrassment? Are there administrative procedures that are immediately implemented in cases of incidents of racial harassment or violence? Are these policies known throughout the institutional community? Are they contained in both student and employee handbooks? Have they been reviewed by legal counsel and local authorities?

5. Does each department or school conduct a periodic assessment of its efforts to improve minority participation and its progress to date?

6. Do schools or units use advisory committees to identify ways to expand contacts in the minority community and to strengthen efforts to recruit minority students, faculty, and administrators? Do they use minority professional associations? minority disciplinary associations? contacts

with deans and department heads at historically black institutions?

7. Does institutional publicity portray minorities in a manner consistent with the goals of enhancing minority participation? Is there a process for reviewing publications and advising on their compatibility with institutional goals?

8. Are employment practices and advancement procedures reviewed periodically to assess their impact on minority faculty and staff? Do special efforts and programs exist to identify promising minority professionals and to assist in their career advancement?

DISSEMINATION AND FOLLOW-UP

The data should be broadly disseminated throughout the institution through a published report as well as hearings and meetings. A presidential address to the entire college community is an effective way to launch the process of formulating or reformulating the institutional agenda.

A self-assessment provides a history, noting progress and failures to date, as well as a point of departure. The remaining chapters outline issues and strategies to consider as you proceed in working on specific areas; checklists at the end of each chapter will assist you in pinpointing problem areas and in monitoring your progress along the way.

SAMPLE WORKSHEET A-1
Scope: *Institution*
Category: *Governing Board*

		Racial and Ethnic Categories (by Sex)									
		White		Black		Hispanic*		Amer. Indian		Asian*	
		Men	Women	Men	Women	Men	Women	Men	Women	Men	Women
	1988										
TOTAL MEM-BERS	1983										
	1978										

*These categories may be further disaggregated, e.g. Puerto Rican, Mexican American, Japanese-American, Chinese-American, and Pacific Islander.

SAMPLE WORKSHEET A-2
Scope: *Institution* **Category:** *Faculty*

		Racial and Ethnic Categories (by Sex)									
		White		Black		Hispanic*		Amer. Indian		Asian*	
		Men	Women	Men	Women	Men	Women	Men	Women	Men	Women
TOTAL	1988										
	1983										
	1978										
FULL-TIME	1988										
	1983										
	1978										
PART-TIME	1988										
	1983										
	1978										
PRO-FESSOR	1988										
	1983										
	1978										
ASSOC. PROF.	1988										
	1983										
	1978										
ASST. PROF.	1988										
	1983										
	1978										
INSTR.	1988										
	1983										
	1978										
TEN-URED	1988										
	1983										
	1978										
NON-TEN-URED	1988										
	1983										
	1978										

*These categories may be further disaggregated, e.g. Puerto Rican, Mexican American, Japanese-American, Chinese-American, and Pacific Islander.

SAMPLE WORKSHEET A-3
Scope: *Institution* **Category:** *Undergraduate Students*

		Racial and Ethnic Categories (by Sex)									
		White		Black		Hispanic*		Amer. Indian		Asian*	
		Men	Women	Men	Women	Men	Women	Men	Women	Men	Women
TOTAL	1988										
	1983										
	1978										
FULL-TIME	1988										
	1983										
	1978										
PART-TIME	1988										
	1983										
	1978										
18-24 YRS.	1988										
	1983										
	1978										
ADULT STU-DENTS	1988										
	1983										
	1978										
RESI-DENT	1988										
	1983										
	1978										
COM-MUTER	1988										
	1983										
	1978										

*These categories may be further disaggregated, e.g. Puerto Rican, Mexican American, Japanese-American, Chinese-American, and Pacific Islander.

SAMPLE WORKSHEET B-1

Scope: *College of Arts and Sciences* **Category:** *Graduate Students*

		Racial and Ethnic Categories (by Sex)									
		White		Black		Hispanic*		Amer. Indian		Asian*	
		Men	Women	Men	Women	Men	Women	Men	Women	Men	Women
TOTAL	1988										
	1983										
	1978										
FULL-TIME	1988										
	1983										
	1978										
PART-TIME	1988										
	1983										
	1978										
TEACH-ING ASSIS-TANTS	1988										
	1983										
	1978										
RE-SEARCH ASSIST-ANTS	1988										
	1983										
	1978										

*These categories may be further disaggregated, e.g. Puerto Rican, Mexican American, Japanese-American, Chinese-American, and Pacific Islander.

SAMPLE WORKSHEET B-2
Scope: *College of Arts and Sciences* **Category:** *Professional Staff**

		Racial and Ethnic Categories (by Sex)									
		White		Black		Hispanic**		Amer. Indian		Asian**	
		Men	Women	Men	Women	Men	Women	Men	Women	Men	Women
TOTAL	1988										
	1983										
	1978										
FULL-TIME	1988										
	1983										
	1978										
PART-TIME	1988										
	1983										
	1978										

*Note: Each institution will need to define the members of a particular category in conformity with its personnel policies and practices.
**These categories may be further disaggregated, e.g. Puerto Rican, Mexican American, Japanese-American, Chinese-American, and Pacific Islander.

SAMPLE WORKSHEET C

Scope: *College of Business* **Dept:** *Management* **Category:** *Faculty*

		Racial and Ethnic Categories (by Sex)									
		White		Black		Hispanic*		Amer. Indian		Asian*	
		Men	Women	Men	Women	Men	Women	Men	Women	Men	Women
TOTAL	1988										
	1983										
	1978										
FULL-TIME	1988										
	1983										
	1978										
PART-TIME	1988										
	1983										
	1978										
PRO-FESSOR	1988										
	1983										
	1978										
ASSOC. PROF.	1988										
	1983										
	1978										
ASST. PROF.	1988										
	1983										
	1978										
INSTR.	1988										
	1983										
	1978										
TEN-URED	1988										
	1983										
	1978										
NON-TEN-URED	1988										
	1983										
	1978										

*These categories may be further disaggregated, e.g. Puerto Rican, Mexican American, Japanese-American, Chinese-American, and Pacific Islander.

3

Undergraduate Students

Recruiting and retaining minority undergraduates are essential to ensuring equity for minority citizens and to improving the learning environment for all students. A college degree provides increased employment opportunity as well as enhanced social standing. Anything less than full access for all citizens to this important credential is clearly unjust. Equally important is the impact of a homogenous campus on all students; an educational experience that does not reflect the pluralism of our country and the importance of minority individuals and cultures is simply deficient.

THE CURRENT SITUATION

High school graduation rates for all Americans have increased since 1976. According to U.S. Census data, for blacks, the percentage of 18 to 24 year olds who have completed high school has risen steadily from 62 percent in 1971 to 71 percent in 1981 and again to 76 percent in 1985. The graduation rate for Hispanics has also improved: it increased from 52 to 56 percent from 1971 to 1981 and then to 63 percent in 1985. But whites are still far ahead, with a graduation rate of nearly 84 percent in 1985, up from slightly over 81 percent in 1971.

There the good news for minority students stops, for the trend does not carry through higher education for them. College attendance by whites has shown modest increases between 1970 and 1985: in 1970, 53 percent of white high school graduates 24 years old or younger were enrolled in or had completed one or more years of college; that percentage rose to 55 percent in 1985. In 1970, 39 percent of black high school graduates were enrolled in or had completed one year of college. That figure rose to 48 percent in 1975 and declined to 44 percent in 1985. The rate of attendance for

Figure 1: Who Goes to College*

*Percent of persons 24 years and younger enrolled or who have completed one or more years of college, by race and Hispanic origin.

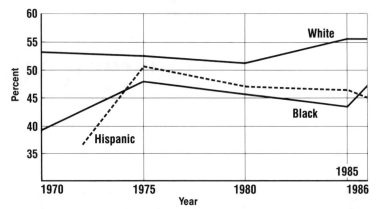

Sources: U.S. Bureau of the Census, *Current Population Reports,* Series P-20, No. 404 (Washington, D.C.: November 1985), Table B: 4, and No. 409 (September 1986), Table 6: 9; also, "School Enrollment—Social and Economic Characteristics of Students: October 1986," forthcoming report.

Hispanic youths declined from 51 to 47 percent during that decade. Recently released 1986 data shows that black attendance has risen to 47 percent, but Hispanic attendance has dropped to 45 percent. The gap in attendance rates of Hispanic and white students is widening.

A major trouble spot is graduation rates. Minority undergraduates are simply not graduating at the same rate as their white counterparts. As Table 1 shows, blacks and Hispanics are far less likely than whites to attain a baccalaureate or master's degree.

Retention, then, must be a priority. Parity between the proportion of minority baccalaureate holders and their share of the population is a reasonable goal for higher education. Closing that gap is imperative.

Table 1: Highest Educational Degree Attained by 1980 H.S. Seniors by Spring 1986

(percentage distribution)

	Assoc. Degree	Bacc. Degree	Master's Degree
Hispanic	7.3	6.8	.1
American Indian	9.3	10.8	.0
Asian	8.7	27.3	1.7
Black	5.3	10.0	.2
White	6.6	20.2	.9

Source: U.S. Department of Education, Center for Education Statistics, Longitudinal Studies Branch, "Highest Degree Attained by 1980 High School Seniors by Sex, Race, Type of Community and Type of High School, as of Spring, 1986," Tabulation LSB 87-09-20, September 20, 1987.

The third area of concern is the unequal distribution of minorities across the disciplines. Although the heavy concentration of blacks and Hispanics in the fields of education and social sciences is beginning to lessen, there are still insufficient numbers of black and Hispanic students majoring in science and mathematics. Ironically, despite their concentration in education, we still have a shortage of minority teachers in primary and secondary schools.

Finally, the issue of competition for the best and the brightest minority students plagues our admissions efforts. Many colleges are engaged in a bidding war for these academic stars, but pay less attention to recruiting average students, or cultivating below-average performers who could be solid students. Enlarging the pool of eligible college students is the only long term strategy that can address the problem of underrepresentation of minority students.

STRATEGIES

What can we do to eliminate the gap between access and completion rates of minorities in higher education? The strategies described here and the programs illustrating these strategies have been gathered from institutions that are successfully addressing this issue. Some of the programs are similar and have been adapted to many institutional settings. The availability of outcome data for the various programs is indicated at the end of each description in this and all subsequent chapters. Below are five types of intervention strategies to bring more minority students into the classroom and improve their retention.

Preparation— Expanding the Pool

College students are recruited from different sources. First, high schools provide an obvious pool. Second, many institutions are increasing their emphasis on adult students who come to college for a variety of reasons—enrichment, job advancement, or retraining. Third, two-year institutions are often overlooked as important preparation grounds for baccalaureate students. They are especially important because of the high concentration of minority students.

The components of our educational system, from kindergarten through graduate school, are highly interdependent. Blaming inadequate preparation on the elementary schools is no substitute for colleges and universities working with school districts serving high proportions of minority students to develop programs to strengthen curriculum, staff, and support services. The following suggestions do not stand alone, of course. They should be considered, as all other strategies recommended in this *Handbook,* in conjunction with the total institutional effort, as well as specific strategies to address other dimensions of the issue. Readers are also encouraged to refer to the following chapter on graduate and professional students; many of the strategies recommended there are also applicable to undergraduate students; some are listed in both chapters.

■ ***Begin with a recruiting plan.*** The point of departure for increasing the numbers and the success rate of minority students (as with all other aspects of minority participation) is a plan. Institutions such as the University of Wisconsin, Ohio State University, and Wayne State University have specified numerical goals and timetables necessary to achieve the goals of their plan. The plan should include a statement of purpose, objectives, implementation strategies, evaluation methods, and a mechanism for revising the plans as objectives are met or fail to be met.

■ ***Work cooperatively with public schools to diagnose and correct the conditions that inhibit the achievement of many students.*** An important element of recruiting minority undergraduates is reaching students as early as elementary school. Increasing students' chances for success before they get to high school can help create a larger pool of students who may think more seriously about going to college. Success breeds self-confidence.

Many institutions are finding that collaboration in projects involving specific disciplines is the most fruitful approach. For example, the engineering faculty can work with junior high and high school mathematics and science teachers to ensure that the pre-college curriculum prepares students to succeed in a collegiate engineering program. Also, such collaborative efforts can develop programs for teachers, students, and parents to encourage interest in science, math, and engineering. Some areas for collaboration between college faculty and K–12 teachers include:

• *Development of pre-college curriculum that will prepare students for college-level coursework.*

- *Development of assessment instruments to assist students in identifying academic weaknesses and to improve student achievement at all levels before college.*

- *Adaptation of junior high and high school curricula to college entry requirements.*

- *Provision of early information about college for junior high and high school students.* This information can be disseminated by admissions officers responsible for recruiting, and by faculty. Collaboration with K–12 counterparts provides college faculty a link to students and the potential for capturing their interest in specific fields of study. Periodic "open houses" hosted by colleges and universities can help motivate junior high and high school students, and make college seem more accessible.

- *Development of weekend and summer programs for minority youth, especially programs with a disciplinary focus.* Some colleges have used team teaching with both college and high school faculty for these courses.

- *College faculty and administrators work with high school guidance counselors to improve guidance programs.*

- *Credit for college students who serve as tutors to primary and secondary school students.*

- *Regular meetings between high school and college instructors within the same discipline to improve communication, knowledge of requirements, and expectations at the college level.*

- *Workshops for high school teachers to share the latest research in teaching.*

- *Area businesses and public schools expose students to the world of work and educational requirements.*

- *Outreach programs to parents of middle, junior high, and even grade school students to orient them to opportunities for their children and how to take advantage of them.* If possible, these programs should be conducted in the language of the parents.

- *Recognition of faculty who participate in these activities.*

This point is central to all the activities suggested in this *Handbook*. Though the intrinsic rewards may be significant, changing one's behavior usually requires incentives or the threat of sanctions. Thus, incentives are vital to encouraging college faculty to participate in such cooperative activities. As long as publications and research are the overwhelming criteria for promotion and tenure, activities such as those described above will hold a distant third place. Recognition for outreach activity and course design in the tenure process can be key incentives. Release time and summer stipends are also well-recognized as effective incentives. Also, the creation of standing groups or working committees will enhance the potential for cooperation at the institutional, college, or even departmental level, and will legitimize these activities for interested faculty as well as provide encouragement.

■ *Develop cooperative arrangements with local community colleges.* Many of the strategies described above will help develop a working relationship with community colleges and their students. Efforts that expose community college students to the programs of four-year institutions can heighten their interest in pursuing their education and make the prospect less formidable. The importance of articulation agreements cannot be overemphasized. In some states, policies applying to transfer from community colleges to public four-year institutions are clearly spelled out. When these agreements are not in place, students need to know which courses are acceptable for transfer credit. Well-crafted agreements involving faculty of the institutions' corresponding departments are essential to smooth articulation.

■ *Consider new populations of students.* Adults are returning to college in great numbers, compensating for the downturn in the 18- to 24-year-old cohort.

Working adults may return to school for many reasons, and outreach to these students through their employers can be highly effective. Also, unemployed persons may seek to develop career skills. Flexible scheduling of courses and support services, designing degree programs to fit a particular community need, are all well recognized in the world of adult and continuing education. Texas Women's University has created an unusual program to provide housing and services for families, most of which are composed of single mothers with children (see below for a description).

Recruiting

Effective recruiting is a critical element of student affirmative action efforts in most colleges and universities, reaching beyond the existing pool of highly qualified minority students and searching out other students who may need more academic and personal support to succeed in college. The following recommendations summarize some strategies used by successful institutions:

- *Give careful attention to local schools.* In urban areas, local high schools offer a large potential pool of minority students. However, students from these high schools are more likely than their white or affluent counterparts to be underprepared. Thus, successful recruiting efforts are made in concert with programs that improve student preparation with the understanding that, once admitted, these students may still need extra help in order to succeed. Some institutions use high-achieving minority students and minority alumni to assist in recruiting. Contacts with local churches and community organizations can also assist recruitment efforts.

- *Four-year institutions and community colleges work collaboratively.* As mentioned above, common calendars, equivalent courses, sound advising, bridge programs, transfer agreements, and similar strategies can facilitate the recruitment and enrollment of minority students in baccalureate programs. It is especially helpful if transfer agreements are course-specific, so that students are not required to repeat courses unnecessarily. It is also advisable that transfer agreements be *degree*-specific, so that the integrity of the associate degree is such that it assures students of being accepted as a junior by the receiving institution.

Four-year institutions should consider inner-city community colleges as rich sources of potential students, and work hard at ensuring that transfer is as simple and straightforward as possible.

- *Recognize differences among and within minority groups.* It is important to recognize that different minority groups have different talents, needs, and problems. Also, there are significant differences within minority groups. For example, Asian-Americans generally outperform all other racial and ethnic groups, and are referred to by some as the "model minority." However, recent Asian immigrants with poor English skills may have considerable academic difficulty that goes unrecognized. By the same token, because of the superior performance in math and science, it is easy to stereotype Asian-Americans either as non-English speakers (though they may have several generations of ancestors here) or as deficient in language and communication skills. Similarly, it is crucial to recognize that middle-class black students from competitive high schools have very different backgrounds and problems from their underprepared, inner-city counterparts. The family and church are often important in reaching Hispanic students. Each of these groups brings different issues to a predominantly white campus and needs different kinds of assistance.

- *Develop informational materials in languages other than English.* A number of institutions have found that making materials available to families in their native language, especially Spanish, helps them understand the complicated business of going to college. The decision to go to college is, for many students, a family decision. Other-language materials can be used by church and community groups and involve families and communities in the decision-making process for first-generation college students.

Admissions

- *Consider higher risk minority students.* In considering the records of these students, institutions should first assess the students' academic weaknesses and provide them with remedial courses, learning labs, and other opportunities to correct their deficiencies. This should be done as soon as they matriculate, and before they are placed in academic situations that require skills they do not yet possess. Sometimes, underprepared students can take some remedial courses at the same time that they take regular college-level coursework. Along with corrective course work, underprepared students need tutorial services, career guidance, assistance in learning how to study, and support programs. These services help students understand the need for participating fully in remedial work and can give them needed confidence in their own abilities. These support programs are outlined in the next selection.

- *Use multiple criteria for admissions purposes.* Overreliance on standardized tests may eliminate black and Hispanic students who do not perform well on tests. Institutions have long recognized the usefulness of additional criteria for admissions, such as musical or athletic ability, or an applicant's status as the child of an alumnus/ae. To recruit able minority students, institutions should consider such factors as grade point average, community service, leadership record, essays, and interviews.

- **Assist minority applicants in admissions procedures.** Many students and their families, and especially first-generation college students, find the application procedures confusing and intimidating. Certainly, financial aid application forms are difficult for students and their parents. Adult students can be equally overwhelmed by the paperwork. Assistance in navigating the admissions and financial aid process can make a real difference in a student's decision to attend college. (The *Strategies* on Admissions in Chapter 4, pp. 61-64, provide additional relevant discussion and suggestions.)

Retention: Student Support Services

Student support services, especially those designed for minority and low income students, have been the principal institutional response to the problems minority students experience in predominantly white institutions. Too often, they have isolated both minority students and the faculty and staff that work with them, thereby "ghettoizing" their participants and contributing to their marginal status on campus. Institutions that have had the most success with support services find that they assist minority students in both their academic and social adaptation to the institution. These services are accessible to all students, comprehensive rather than fragmented or sporadic. The following strategies are recommended:

- **Create a hospitable environment for minority students.** Minority students, both high-risk students and those with strong academic credentials, often find themselves—for the first time—in an environment that is predominantly, even overwhelmingly, white. Students accustomed to predominantly minority secondary schools may have to look hard to find a friendly black or brown face. Certainly, the more minority students on campus, the less conspicuous and isolated individual minority group members will feel. Programs and activities to ease their transition, such as summer programs for high school students, orientation programs for all students, peer counselors, and social and cultural opportunities that expose all students to cultural diversity will help minority students feel more comfortable and welcome and contribute to the education of all students.

A grievance process to address incidents of racial or ethnic discrimination, harrassment, or assaults, and a designated, accessible individual to deal with complaints and grievances, are also important. Programs to sensitize majority students and faculty and reduce campus conflict are essential.

■ *Demonstrate the importance of support services.* Successful institutions incorporate services for minority students into related services for all students. They involve many individuals from all parts of the institution in ensuring minority student success. They ensure that each individual to whom students may turn for assistance has all the necessary information to prevent students from being shunted from one office to another.

Some colleges and universities rely exclusively on external funds for special services. This practice sends a message to staff and students that they are not central to the institution's purpose. Institutions are also encouraged to lodge responsibility for minority students with staff members who are an integral part of the student or academic services staff. This practice encourages all faculty and staff to take an active role or have a personal stake in the success of minority students. It also prevents the isolation of students, faculty, and staff in these special service areas.

Academic Support Programs

Colleges and universities need coherent academic strategies to work with students they admit. That is, they need to develop a plan that ties together recruitment, academic, and student support services, as well as financial aid services. These strategies begin with the coordination of course competencies between high schools and colleges, and extend through relationships between two- and four-year institutions. They should address—at all levels—the needs of students who require academic remediation and support services. Institutions that have worked with significant numbers of underprepared minority students have employed a number of strategies:

- *Emphasize teaching and learning for all students.* As Chapter 8 explains, an institution-wide commitment to effective teaching and student progress will benefit all students, but especially those who are underprepared or insecure in their environments. College and universities can expect to have their minority students graduate if they expect all students to achieve, give sustained attention to correcting deficiencies in students' academic backgrounds, monitor their progress regularly, and provide counseling and support programs.

- *Relate support programs to academic majors.* Effective support programs have several characteristics. They assess all incoming students to determine if they meet criteria for success in college-level courses. Those judged as deficient enter developmental sequences in math, writing, reading, and study skills, from which they exit by achieving specified competencies. These competencies are identified by the faculty of the student's academic major, not developmental program faculty. Many institutions have found it advisable to place developmental courses under the purview of the academic faculty. At the same time, the faculty may need special assistance and training in helping students to correct their deficiencies.

- *Provide trained, experienced teachers for underprepared students.* Underprepared students need the most effective teachers. Special training for the academic faculty is often required to help them understand how to be most effective teaching students with academic deficiencies.

- *Integrate academic support programs with student service counterparts.* Like majority students, minority students need support groups, tutorial services, academic advising, and career counseling. These services should be mutually supportive and internally consistent.

- *Provide peer counseling.* Peer counseling is an effective and nonthreatening way to assist minority students in understanding and confronting academic and social problems.

- *Provide an "early warning system."* Freshmen students in trouble must be identified early and helped before it is too late. Faculty members may need training on how to identify poor achievers, and then convince them to call upon academic support.

Some institutions have automatic procedures to refer students from faculty to counselors when they show signs of academic difficulties during the first year. Counseling for underprepared, first-generation college students is often more aggressive and provides more direction than ordinary student counseling. Fifty percent of minority student attrition occurs in the first year of college; so an early warning system is particularly important.

Also, some institutions require that students see their counselors on a regular basis and schedule it into their programs. Another approach is a one-credit freshman seminar on study skills and adjustment to college life, including discussion of cultural differences.

Financial Aid

A critical aspect of student enrollment and retention is financial aid. This does not simply refer to providing grants and loans for needy students. Counseling and planning assistance are also critical to helping needy students manage their money and plan ahead. For poor students, adequate funds for school may be only a small part of their overall financial situation. Concern over the family's financial situation may contribute to the student's dropping out. The following practices should be helpful to students requiring financial aid:

- *Inform the student as early as possible about financial awards—preferably at the time of admission.* Some schools do not inform students of the availability of funds until a few weeks before matriculation. This is inadequate for a family to plan all the strategies necessary to send a child to college or to integrate this burden with other financial commitments. Financially independent students have similar problems and need to plan ahead.

- *Provide more work-study programs and fewer loans to minority students.* For a family with few financial resources, a large loan is a disincentive to send a child to college. It is also an added burden to working adults with families and other debts to pay. Needy students often prefer work-study programs. Financial aid policies should encourage work-study, since many needy students can benefit from the opportunity to earn, rather than borrow. Work-study may also assist in the socialization of minority students.

- *Connect work-study programs to course and workload decisions.* Jobs can often assist students in the selection of a course of study. It is most helpful to students to participate in work programs that are related to their career ambitions. It is also important to note that jobs can interfere with coursework, both by overburdening the student and by conflicting with course requirements. Work-study programs should be connected with counseling services to assure that the work does not interfere with academic progress.

■ *Provide budget counseling and emergency loan services.* Needy students may not understand budgeting. Furthermore, they may be tempted to spend money set aside for education expenses on other family needs. They may need counseling on how to prepare and live within a budget. An emergency loan program for students to draw upon in times of severe financial stress is a useful addition to financial aid services.

CHECKLIST

The sections of the checklist correspond to the sections of this chapter: expanding the pool, recruiting and admissions, academic and student support services, and financial aid. Certainly, not all of the strategies listed in each section will be helpful in all institutions. As with the checklist presented in Chapter 2, the following questions can be applied to each item to assess its value in your particular context:

■ If the answer is *yes*, is the strategy or policy effective? How do you assess how well it is working? What outcome data do you have?

■ If the answer is *no*, would such an approach be useful? How high a priority would you place on developing such a policy or strategy?

Expanding the Pool

Suggested reviewers: admissions staff, faculty, academic administrators.

1. Does the institution have a program to identify potential minority students? Is the program funded separately, or included in the overall commitment of the recruiting and admissions office? How is the program assessed?

2. Has the institution developed working relationships with high schools? Is information readily available outlining institutional entrance requirements? Are support services available to junior and senior high school students to stimulate their interest in higher education?

3. Is there an ongoing relationship between the institution's recruiting personnel and counselors at secondary schools with significant minority student populations? Are the high school counselors completely informed about institutional entrance requirements?

4. Do you have outreach programs to help prepare minority students for college coursework?

5. Are there continuing efforts to assess the effectiveness of various outreach efforts?

6. If you are a four-year institution: Do you have cooperative relationships of any sort with local community colleges? programmatic collaboration? cooperative relationships among the faculty members? Is information about your institution readily available to students at the community college?

7. Do you work with local businesses and community groups to serve their educational needs and those of workers and citizens?

Recruiting and Admissions

Suggested reviewers: Admissions staff, faculty, academic administrators.

1. If you are a four-year institution: Are there articulation agreements with community colleges? Do they clearly specify acceptable courses and facilitate easy transition into the four-year program?

2. Are special efforts made to recruit minority students into disciplines in which they are underrepresented?

3. Do the information and materials made available to prospective students present an accurate picture of program requirements and campus life? Are they reviewed by minority individuals?

4. Are recruiting materials and informational services available in foreign languages?

5. Are admissions criteria periodically reviewed to determine their impact on minority candidates?

6. Does the admissions process distinguish between those students admitted under standard admissions criteria and those students admitted as academically high risk? Is there an automatic referral to counseling services for high-risk students?

Academic and Student Support Services

Suggested reviewers: Faculty, advisors, student affairs personnel.

1. Are academic advisors assigned to minority students sensitive to their personal and academic needs? Do they receive special training for this purpose? Is the effectiveness of student advising regularly reviewed?

2. Does the freshman orientation program recognize the special needs of minority students?

3. Is there an early warning system to identify students with academic difficulties? Are active interventions made?

4. Is the academic progress of minority students studied to determine which factors contribute to their success or failure?

5. Are students assessed before course enrollments to assure appropriate course placements? Are remedial services readily available without stigma?

6. Are remedial courses taught by instructors expert in the field? Are faculty rewarded for such teaching?

7. Is peer counseling available to minority students? How are counselors selected? trained? evaluated?

Financial Aid

Suggested reviewers: Admissions and financial aid staff.

1. Are the financial aid packages offered to low-income minority students adequate to the students' real needs?

2. Are institutional funds set aside to supplement aid for low-income minority students? What priority is given to minority students in the distribution of institutional aid dollars? Who makes these decisions?

3. Are efforts made to ensure that low-income minority students are not excessively burdened with loans, and that, whenever possible, they receive grants rather than loans?

4. Are there funds available for emergency loans?

5. Is emphasis given to ensure that campus work assignments complement the student's educational program and career interests? Are there policies or practices to help underprepared minority students in their work assignments through the help of faculty mentors?

6. Are any additional monies available to encourage departments and faculty members to develop meaningful assignments for work-study students?

7. Is special guidance available to financially disadvantaged minority students to provide technical assistance and counseling in budget matters? Is the effectiveness of these services assessed?

8. Are workshops on financial aid offered to high school counselors?

9. Is financial aid information made available to students and their families early in their high school years? Do seniors in high school receive additional information and reminders to apply for financial aid early in their senior years? How is the effectiveness of the information program assessed?

PROGRAMS AND PRACTICES

Developing an Institutional Plan

The Ohio State University. In November 1987, the Office of Academic Affairs developed a comprehensive plan to recruit and retain black students. Based on the results of numerous university studies, especially the work of three faculty, staff, and student task forces, successful ongoing recruitment and retention programs, and the responses of individual members of the university community, it outlines a multidimensional plan. Three major goals are specified:

- To increase the educational attainment among black youth in Ohio and thereby enlarge the pool of eligible and interested black students.

- To increase the accessibility of The Ohio State University (OSU) to black undergraduates through recruitment and retention strategies.

- To create a university environment, enhanced by its diversity, in which each member can engage in the fullest development of his or her talents.

To accomplish these goals, seven objectives were specified:

1. To increase substantially the pool of college-eligible black youth in Ohio by 1994.

2. To increase the OSU enrollment of black first quarter freshmen to at least 440 in 1988, 470 in 1989, 510 in 1990, 575 in 1991, and 650 in 1992–4.

3. To improve the persistence rate of black undergraduate students so that it converges with that for white students.

4. To continue the strong record of recruiting and retaining black graduate and professional students.

5. To develop a plan for increasing the proportion of black and other underrepresented minority faculty and staff in each college and for all administrative units.

6. To designate the administrative leadership for each aspect of the recruitment and retention efforts and to establish monitoring systems for all programs.

7. To enhance the university climate by promoting the value of racial and ethnic diversity and by initiating comprehensive steps to eliminate campus racism.

The report outlines a series of strategies to accomplish each of the objectives and specifies a time for their implementation.
CONTACT: *Barbara Newman, Associate Provost, (614) 292-5881.*

Expanding the Pool and Recruiting

Eastern Michigan's College Day Program. Initiated in 1987, this program targets junior high school minority students, and involves young students and their parents in the college process. In order to be eligible for the program, the student must maintain a 2.0 G.P.A., take college preparation courses, have a 90 percent school attendance rate, and have no discipline problems. If the students are successful in the program, they will be guaranteed admission to Eastern Michigan University, Cleary College, Madonna College, or Washtenaw Community College. If eligible to enroll in Eastern Michigan University, students will be provided with the necessary

financial aid (with no loans) for their first year of college. Periodic visits to the campus are built into the program as a way of developing students' self-esteem and sustaining their excitement about going to college. An evaluation of the program is forthcoming.
CONTACT: *Lynette Findley, Director, MLK-CC-RP College Day Program, (313) 487-2133.*

UCLA Center for Academic Interinstitutional Programs (CAIP), Graduate School of Education. The largest program of university-school-community college cooperation in the country, the CAIP has worked since 1980 to ensure equality in preparation by providing professional development for instructional personnel and by refocusing curriculum. It brings together faculty members and their counterparts in the schools and community colleges to improve both content and pedagogy. The CAIP holds annual summer institutes with extended follow-up for principals, counselors, and teachers of mathematics, language arts, science, literature, humanities, geography, and fine arts. The CAIP is a national center for research in the teaching of history. It is now the center of faculty alliances in history, geography, mathematics, chemistry, biology, political science, and chemical engineering, dedicated to collegial exchange between UCLA and community college faculty. An evaluation of the program is available.
CONTACT: *Juan Lara, Assistant Dean, Graduate School of Education, (213) 825-2531.*

The Career Beginnings Program. This national program involves 25 campuses in a network administered by Brandeis University: Chicago City-Wide Colleges; Columbia College, IL; University of Minnesota; Case Western Reserve University; Passaic County Community College; Indiana University Northwest; University of Rochester; Youngstown State University, OH; Boston area colleges and universities; Hartford Consortium for Higher Education; Bronx Community College; City University of New York Graduate School; Columbia University; Jacksonville University; North Carolina State University; Miami-Dade Community College; Christian Brothers College; Butler University; Bellarmine College; University of Louisville; Des Moines Area Community College, IA; Rancho Santiago College, CA; Fullerton College, CA; California State University Bakersfield; and Tacoma Community College, WA. It consists of a three-way partnership between high schools, colleges, and the private sector and builds on the demonstrated abilities of disadvantaged high school juniors to enable their successful entry into postsecondary education. Program components include: one-to-one adult mentoring, a quality summer work experience, job skills and college application training, and year-long guidance throughout the process of gaining admission to college. Approximately 2,600 students and 2,600 volunteer mentors are involved in the program nationally. On some campuses, students work with student mentors; they receive continued program staff support to insure a smooth transition and facilitate their retention. An evaluation of the program is available.

CONTACT: *Co-directors Erik Payne Butler or Andrew Hahn, Center for Human Resources, Florence Heller Graduate School for Advanced Studies, Brandeis University, (617) 736-3770 or (800) 343-4705.*

Hispanic Mother/Daughter Program, Arizona State University (ASU). Initiated in 1984, this early intervention program aims to increase the number of Hispanic women entering higher education and professional careers. The program is unique in that it brings mother-daughter teams to campus during the eighth grade, before students begin to make academic choices that tend to disqualify them from college entrance. To achieve its goal, 60 mother-daughter teams from five school districts participate annually in the program which includes exercises designed to build self-esteem, exposure to Hispanic women professionals in the community, instructional labs, field trips, and a weekend stay on campus. Students who complete the eighth grade component of the program are monitored academically through high school, and periodic activities in high school are scheduled to maintain the students' interest, motivation, and preparation for college. The program involves a close working relationship between the elementary, high school, community college, and university levels of education which assist both mothers and daughters in their educational career aspirations. Program evaluations are available; the program is funded through ASU and the AT&T Foundation.

CONTACT: *Jo Anna O'Donnell, Associate Dean of Student Life, (602) 965-6547.*

Mathematics, Engineering, Science Achievement (MESA). Twenty-two public and private California colleges and universities participate in MESA. Begun in 1970, the program is designed to prepare pre-college minority students for engineering and other math based careers. The junior high and high school activities include organized study, academic advising, scholarship incentive awards, MESA meetings, career exploration, and family involvement. The college-level MESA Minority Engineering Program also has a center on campus to support minority student engineering organizations, and to make available information on career development and summer jobs.

CONTACT: *Mr. Fred Easter, Statewide Director, (415) 642-5064.*

Pre-College Programs in Engineering and Science, New Jersey Institute of Technology (NJIT). Each year, NJIT conducts approximately 10 programs to introduce, prepare, and motivate young people to choose careers in engineering and science. More than 80 percent of the participants are minority, and half are women; most students are inner-city youngsters from low-income households. The programs serve more than 600 students from grades 4 to 12. The oldest of the programs has completed its 17th year; the newest is one year old. Surveys of program participants show that over 95 percent enroll in college and a high proportion select engineering, computer science, or science. Additional outcome data are available.

CONTACT: *Harold Deutschman, Co-Director, Pre-college Urban Engineering Programs, (201) 596-3550.*

Nizhoni Camp at Northern Arizona University. Initiated in 1974, Nizhoni Camp is designed for Native American high school students who want to pursue a college degree but are lacking the study or social skills necessary for a smooth transition from high school to college. The intensive five-week program has two components: Precollegiate and the Bridge programs. Both consist of English and math classes with an integrated studies course that incorporates reading, study skills, computer literacy, and career exploration. An evaluation of the program is available.

CONTACT: *Tanya Gorman, Assistant Director, Educational Support Program, (602) 523-2761.*

Student/Teacher Educational Partnership (STEP) at UC, Irvine. STEP is a comprehensive model of academic collaboration joining four postsecondary institutions with a local district with 87 percent minority enrollments to improve the student academic preparation. Begun in 1982, STEP addresses curricular revision, professional development, student academic support, and parental involvement. Awards from the National Commission on Excellence, the Carnegie Corporation, and California Academic Partnership Program will assist in dissemination of project models, including new practices in teaching math/science and in developing future teachers. An evaluation of the program is forthcoming. **CONTACT:** *Manuel Gomez, Assistant Vice Chancellor, (714) 856-4804.*

Vassar College Summer Progam for Community College Students. Begun in 1984 in cooperation with LaGuardia Community College, this program now includes four community colleges in New York State—LaGuardia, Borough of Manhattan, Dutchess County and Ulster County—to provide a summer program for majority and minority community college students on the Vassar campus. The program's purpose is to develop students' interest in pursuing a baccalaureate degree. During the five-week residential program, specially designed classes are team-taught by two-year and four-year college faculty members. Students are supported by peer counselors, by an academic counselor, and a writing specialist. One hundred and six students completed the program during the first three years. Nearly all transferred to four-year colleges; 19 attend Vassar and one has graduated. Outcome data are available. **CONTACT:** *Colton Johnson, Dean of Studies, Vassar College, (914) 452-7000 ext. 3142.*

Middle College High School, LaGuardia Community College. Founded in 1974 and located on the campus of LaGuardia Community College in Queens, NY, Middle College High School serves approximately 500 students in the 10th, 11th, and 12th grades who have experienced academic and discipline problems. This alternative high school offers internships for academic credit. The sense of independence and responsibility provided by the college atmosphere is supported by small classes and frequent sessions with guidance counselors. Evaluations are available. **CONTACT:** *Cecilia Cullen, Principal, Middle College High School, (718) 482-5440.*

Student and Academic Support Programs

Minority Engineering Program (MEP), Purdue University. Initiated in 1974, MEP includes summer workshops designed to motivate junior and senior high school students to pursue a career in engineering. Once enrolled in the Engineering School, individual and career guidance sessions are available, as are orientation and retention seminars, awards, and information on employment opportunities and scholarships. An evaluation of the program is forthcoming.
CONTACT: *Marion W. Blalock, Director, (317) 494-3974.*

The University of Wisconsin–Madison has a similar program, in operation 13 years.
CONTACT: *Al Hampton or Naomi Walton Winfield, (608) 262-7764.*

Winthrop College. Concern about the declining minority student population on campus motivated Winthrop College to initiate a comprehensive program in 1981 to recruit and retain minority students. Programs designed to offer individualized counseling to assist students in the successful completion of college work include: Significant Other Student Program, Summer Transitional Educational Program, Administrators Mentoring Program, and Freshmen/Transfer Adjustment Program. Winthrop College now has the highest percentage of full-time minority students of any historically white institution in South Carolina. Evaluations of these programs are available.
CONTACT: *David Belton, Assistant to the President, Affirmative Action Office, (803) 323-2277).*

UCLA Transfer Alliance Program (TAP). Initiated in 1985 by UCLA's Center for Academic Institutional Programs (CAIP), TAP seeks to strengthen academic ties between UCLA and selected community colleges. Academic preparation at the community college is the key to retaining transfer students at UCLA. TAP offers its students an enriched general education core curriculum, designed to include extra writing and research assignments; intensive curricular planning; extracurricular experiences such as visits to museums, libraries, and laboratories; specialized counseling; faculty mentoring; and opportunities to interact with UCLA students and faculty. Minority students are encouraged to enroll, since TAP helps to create a peer group based on academic excellence, which contributes toward retention and a sense of the intellectual

rigor required for a successful transition. Successful TAP graduates are guaranteed priority admission to UCLA's College of Letters and Science. Freshmen applicants not admitted to UCLA are encouraged to enroll in TAP and transfer as juniors. UCLA encourages high school counselors to recommend TAP as an alternative entrance to UCLA. An evaluation, funded by Ford Foundation and UCLA, is forthcoming.
CONTACT: *Gayle J. Byock, (213) 825-7053.*

College Assistance Migrant Program (CAMP), California State University, Fresno. Since 1981, the CAMP project has served as a retention program for students of migrant and seasonal farmworkers. It recognizes that the students' high school preparation and family backgrounds tend to put them at a higher risk of failure than other first-time college students; thus, the program addresses the students' study skill deficiencies, language development, and career planning skills. An evaluation of the program is available.
CONTACT: *Raul Z. Diaz, Director, (209) 294-4768.*

Grambling State University. Focusing on retention as the key to increasing enrollment, in 1981 Grambling instituted a highly structured comprehensive developmental educational program. The main components are a laboratory and special tutoring in remedial reading, mathematics, and English, and an organized and trained staff in the Academic Skills Center. The institution credits the program with increasing enrollment for nine consecutive semesters. An evaluation of the program is available.
CONTACT: *Dr. Lamore J. Carter, (318) 274-2291.*

Faculty Mentor Program, California State University, Sacramento. Since its inception in 1987, the program has trained 10 percent of the full-time faculty at California State University, Sacramento to serve as mentors to 300 first-time freshmen and transfer students from historically underrepresented ethnic groups. The faculty has participated in training sessions which cover such topics as "Barriers to Cross-Cultural Communication" and "Underrepresented Students' Expectations of CSU, Sacramento Faculty." The program is designed to help students develop greater understanding of university life and the opportunities it presents.
CONTACT: *Dr. Isabel Hernandez-Serna, (916) 278-6331.*

Counseling and Academic Skills Development (CASD), Pennsylvania State University. The CASD program is designed to provide individualized counseling and academic support services for minority undergraduates with top priority given to at-risk freshmen students. Counseling services include classroom skill improvement, career planning, financial aid and money management, university policy and regulations, and interpersonal relations with peers and family. An evaluation of the program is forthcoming.
CONTACT: *Marc B. Levey, (814) 865-1771.*

Minority Professional Opportunities (MPO), Illinois State University. This program was developed in 1984 for highly talented minority students whose standardized test scores reflect potential academic success. The program provides a two-day summer orientation program for freshmen and their parents, a one-credit orientation class designed to facilitate the transition from high school to college, and a series of MPO activities throughout the year. It also provides students with personal and academic counseling and information about graduate schools, as well as possible professional opportunities. Other opportunities include paid and unpaid mentorship experiences, career choice classes, trips to graduate and professional schools, and conferences and job fairs.
CONTACT: *Francene Gilmer, MPO Director, (309) 438-7641.*

Indiana University (IU) Northwest's Special Services Project. Indiana University Northwest has the highest minority enrollment of all the IU regional campuses. The year-round services provided by the Special Services Staff to eligible students include tutoring, counseling, seminars in study skills, goal setting, time managemet, and cultural enrichment, with special instruction in an eight-week summer component to prepare students for the competitive Nursing and Allied Health career programs. An evaluation of the program is forthcoming.
CONTACT: *Barbara Cope, Vice Chancellor, (291) 980-6702.*

University of Wisconsin-Oshkosh Early Warning/Intervention Program. This computerized data-driven program consists of three phases: (1) High Risk Prediction, (2) Early Alert, and (3) Intervention. To initiate Phase I, a computer program scans the Student Master File data for incoming freshmen and evaluates that data against established criteria to generate a list of Early Warning Notification (EWN) forms. Phase

II monitors the academic progress of identified high risk students enrolled in designated preparatory and basic courses. During the first week of the semester, forms are sent to the faculty teaching these identified courses, requesting information on the performance of the students after three weeks. Data is compiled and reviewed, and referred to Academic Development Services to initiate Intrusive Advisory/ Intervention. The advisor contacts and meets with each student to provide academic counseling, referral to the peer tutor program, and to suggest other forms of assistance. This program has shown a steady increase in student retention rates, with over 70 percent of students remaining in college. Evaluation data available.
CONTACT: *Linda Huang, Coordinator, (414) 424-3080.*

Texas Women's University, Family Housing and Services. Growing demands for on-campus housing by married and single-parent students at the university resulted in the decision in 1982 to convert a residence hall to family housing (efficiency and 2-bedroom apartments) over a five-year period. Many residents are single mothers with children who juggle several roles (parent, student, "sole breadwinner"). Resources and programs are presented on family relations, parenting, self-concept, study skills, stress management, and other topics. An after-school recreation program for children is also provided.
CONTACT: *Dr. Glenda Brock Simmons, Vice President for Student Life, (817) 898-3676.*

PACE (Peer Advising on the College Experience), Seattle University. Begun in 1986, PACE is a peer advising program intended to assist new minority students in making a smooth transition to Seattle University. PACE utilizes upper-level students to provide academic and social support to address the unique needs of minority students. Peer advisors help new students develop a realistic academic plan, understand school procedures and processes, and access support services. Advisors may also offer tutoring or studying sessions. PACE is designed to help students reduce social isolation through strengthening the relationship between new and current students. Peer advisors, in return, receive financial assistance and the opportunity to develop leadership skills.
CONTACT: *Shelia Hood, Associate Vice President for Enrollment Services, (206) 296-5905.*

Financial Aid

Minority Incentive Scholarship, University of Arkansas at Fayetteville. This scholarship has been awarded since 1983 to selected freshman minority students who satisfy the requirements for traditional admissions but do not qualify for the university's Freshman Academic Scholarship. The award includes the amount of full registration fees and is renewable the following year.
CONTACT: *Vanessa Gladney, Assistant Director of Admissions, (501) 575-5346.*

FASTrack (Financial Aid Security Track Program), University of Wisconsin–Madison. FASTrack is designed to help low-income Wisconsin students pay for college through a combination of grants, work-study, and loans. It is a long-term program intended to let qualified high school students know that if they meet admissions requirements, they will have access to a college education. The program reduces reliance on borrowing and features no borrowing during the freshman year. Financially dependent Wisconsin students will be eligible for the program based on family income and need for assistance to meet college costs. The program, begun in the fall of 1988, will save 150 new freshman each year. Within four years, an estimated 600 students will be served by the program, which assures that student financial needs will be met each year for four years, with a possibility of extension.
CONTACT: *Wallace Douma, Financial Aids Director, (608) 263-3202.*

4

Graduate and Professional Students

*G*raduate and professional schools are critical to increasing minority participation throughout society, for they train the next generation of leaders, not only
in education, but in business and the professions. Today's graduate and professional students are tomorrow's doctors, lawyers, college faculty, administrators,
and role models for the next generation.

THE CURRENT SITUATION

As we follow the continuum of minority participation
in higher education—undergraduate students, graduate students, and faculty—the numbers fall off
distressingly. Black, Hispanic, and American Indian students
are far less well represented in graduate and professional
schools than at the undergraduate level. In 1986, while
blacks comprised 9.2 percent of undergraduates, they ac-
counted for only 5 percent of graduate and first professional
degree students. Hispanics comprised 5.3 percent of undergraduates, but only approximately 3 percent of graduate and
first professional enrollments. American Indians represented
.8 percent of undergraduate enrollments, but .4 percent of
graduate and professional students.

The trends of the past decade in the number of minority students enrolling in graduate and professional schools has var-
ied among different minority groups. Between 1976 and
1986, the number of minority students in graduate school
grew by nearly 40 percent, while white enrollments grew by
10 percent. The number of Hispanic and Asian graduate students more than doubled, while the number of black students
did not increase at all. These increases are encouraging, but
absolute numbers are still small: there were 46,000 Hispanic,
72,000 black and 5,000 American Indian graduate students

enrolled in 1986, comprising, respectively, 3.2, 5.0, and 0.4 percent of all graduate students. Similar increases were registered for enrollments of some minority groups in professional schools. Between 1976 and 1986, white enrollments in professional schools grew by 5 percent, while minority enrollments increased by over 70 percent. Hispanic and Asian enrollments doubled, while black enrollments increased by a more modest, but still encouraging, 25 percent. The numbers of black and Hispanic graduate and professional students are still insufficient to achieve adequate representation in the professions and in faculty positions.

A look at the actual numbers of doctoral degrees granted leaves little doubt that unless we increase the numbers of minority doctoral candidates, the problem of a limited faculty pool will persist. As the table below indicates, in 1976, 1,213 blacks were awarded doctorates; 11 years later in 1987, that number dropped to 904, according to recently released data from the National Research Council. While the number of doctorates granted to white students also dropped, from approximately 27,400 in 1976 to 21,000 in 1987, the share of doctorates awarded to blacks still declined from 3.6 to 2.8 percent. The proportion and number of black men receiving doctorates is falling, from 3.0 percent of all doctorates in 1976 to 2.6 percent in 1986.

Doctorates awarded to Hispanics nearly doubled in number—but from only 396 in 1976 to 709 in 1987. During that same period, the number of Asian doctorate recipients rose to 1,162 from 583 and American Indian rose from 93 to 115.

The unequal distribution of minority students across the disciplines poses another serious problem. The National Research Council reports that over 40 percent of all doctorates awarded to blacks in 1987 were in education, as were 30 percent of doctorates awarded to Hispanics. Nationally, only 20 percent of doctoral degrees awarded were in education that year.

Shortages of minority doctorate holders in science, mathematics, and engineering are acute. Among the 3,341 doctorates awarded in the United States in 1987 to U.S. citizens and permanent visa residents in the physical sciences, 35 (1%) went to blacks, 76 (2%) to Hispanics, 228 (7%) to Asians, and 10 to American Indians. Similarly, of the 1,908 doctorates awarded to citizens and permanent visa holders in engineering, 25 (1%) went to blacks, 34 (2%) to Hispanics, 326 (17%) to Asians, and 7 to American Indians.

Table 2: Total Doctorate Degrees by Race/Ethnicity for Selected Years

	1975-76		1984-85		1986-87*	
	total	percent	total	percent	total	percent
All	33,787	100.0	32,307	100.0	32,278	100.0
Men	26,010	77.0[1]	21,296	65.9	20,908	64.8
Women	7,777	23.0[2]	11,011	34.1	11,370	35.2
Minority	2,285	6.8[3]	3,056	9.5	2,790	
Men	1,167	6.2[4]	1,856	8.7		
Women	668	8.6[5]	1,198	10.9		
Hispanic	396	1.2	677	2.1	709	
Men	289	1.1	431	2.0		
Women	107	1.4	246	2.2		
Black	1,213	3.6	1,154	3.6	804	
Men	771	3.0	561	2.6		
Women	442	5.7	593	5.4		
White	27,434	81.2	23,934	74.1	21,007	
Men	20,852	80.2	15,017	70.5		
Women	6,582	84.6	8,917	80.0		
Asian/Pacific Islander	583	1.7	1,106	3.4	1,162	
Men	480	1.8	802	3.8		
Women	103	1.3	304	2.8		
Amer. Indian	93	0.3	119	0.4	115	
Men	77	0.3	64	0.3		
Women	16	0.2	55	0.5		
Non-resident alien	4,068	12.0	5,317	16.5	5,593	
Men	3,541	13.6	4,421	20.8		
Women	527	6.8	896	8.1		

Notes:
[1] Degrees awarded to men as a percentage of all doctorate degrees awarded that year.
[2] Degrees awarded to women as a percentage of all doctorate degrees awarded that year.
[3] Degrees awarded to this group as a percentage of all doctorate degrees awarded that year. [4] Degrees awarded to men this group as a percentage of all doctorate degrees awarded to men that year. [5] Degrees awarded to women in this group as a percentage of all doctorate degrees to women awarded that year.

Source: *Minorities in Higher Education: Sixth Annual Status Report.* American Council on Education, 1987. p. 21.
*Source: National Research Council, *1987 Survey of Earned Doctorates,* preliminary data.

STRATEGIES

T he representation of graduate and professional students on campuses can be improved through a number of interventions: the applicant pool can be increased; recruitment intensified; adequate financial aid provided to ensure that financial need is not an insuperable barrier; and the campus can be supportive of the needs of minority students through the development of programs and structures conducive to their success. Many of the issues and strategies related to increasing minority graduate and professional school enrollment are similar to those aimed at recruiting and retaining undergraduate students. Readers should refer to the preceding chapter on undergraduate students for additional relevant information.

Preparation— Expanding the Pool

The most important initiative that graduate and professional schools can take to increase minority enrollment is to cultivate and enlarge the pool of potential students. It is a long-term initiative, not conducive to instant results. Nevertheless, a strong effort to increase the pool will pay off in attracting and retaining minority graduate and professional students. Successful institutions suggest the following strategies:

- *Recruit "at home."* The most accessible population of minorities to consider for graduate and professional school should be the university's own population of undergraduates and recent graduates.

- *Inform minority undergraduates of the rewards of graduate study.* Developing programs to make undergraduate students aware of graduate study, its use for job prospects, and its merit in preparing students for fulfilling careers, can help identify talented students and give them needed encouragement to pursue further study. Such awareness programs should be in place at home as well as at "feeder schools," including regional colleges and community colleges with substantial minority enrollments.

- *Reach minority students early in their undergraduate careers.* Through relationships with undergraduate institutions, and with their own undergraduate students, counsel students about requirements for specific coursework and graduate program entrance requirements.

In counseling minority students, it is important to make them aware of fields that accept students from a variety of undergraduate majors. Minority students who major in ethnic studies or other nontraditional fields may need help choosing graduate programs that do not require them to concentrate in a specific undergraduate major. These students can be encouraged to pursue law, business administration, interdisciplinary studies, and similar graduate programs. This approach also permits them to pursue personal interests at the undergraduate level without cutting off the possibility of graduate preparation.

- *Provide role models from minority racial and ethnic groups.* Minority students need role models to motivate and inspire them to envision a future for themselves as professionals, researchers or university professors. Most predominantly white campuses do not have a racially diverse faculty. However, they can take immediate action to recruit minority speakers and visiting professors, as well as make a long-term commitment to hiring more permanent minority faculty. Many institutions invite minority graduate and professional school alumni to address undergraduates. Interested retired minority faculty can become emissaries who contact prospective minority graduate students.

- *Provide opportunities for minority undergraduates to pursue academic research under the tutelage of graduate student and faculty mentors.* This approach provides a first-hand introduction to the rewards and importance of academic research and can motivate students to pursue academic careers.

- *Identify minority individuals who have left campus and may want to continue their education.* The pool of potential graduate and professional students can be expanded by contacting minority alumni who are now in business, industry, government, or education and may want to go on to graduate work. For these efforts to be successful in the long run, however, it is important that class schedules, financial aid, and program structure be responsive to the needs of working, part-time graduate students.

- *Work with employers in industry, government, and the nonprofit sector to identify needs and interests in graduate study.* Working adults interested in pursuing graduate as well as undergraduate education need special attention on two fronts. First, employers may be interested in the creation of special programs (degree or non-degree), or in the adaptation of existing programs to fit their particular needs. Adaptations for adult students, such as bringing courses to the work site or changing scheduling to fit their needs, may be a crucial factor in their decisions.

Recruitment

As with undergraduate students, effective recruiting of minority graduate and professional school students involves reaching beyond the obvious pool and taking an active role in tapping new sources of students. Every institution can enter the competition for the minority "superstars," but there is more promising talent than those few individuals. Here are some strategies that have been successful:

- *Expand the "old boy" network.* The graduate faculty network often excludes minority faculty members and faculty members at colleges with large numbers of minority students. Yet undergraduate college faculty members tend to be the most influential persons in students' decisions to attend graduate and professional school.

Faculty members—particularly those with responsibilities for graduate programs—can acquaint themselves with faculty members at colleges with potential minority graduate students. This can be done through exchange programs, attending meetings of disciplinary associations, and visiting their campuses. The graduate school can finance the costs of adding an extra day to a faculty member's trip to a conference or professional meeting to enable him or her to visit these campuses and meet with faculty and potential graduate students. Faculty who are successful at recruiting minority students create the expectation that minority students are viable candidates for graduate study and that they can succeed. Expectations of success breed success.

- *Institute student visitation programs.* Minority students can visit the graduate and professional programs at university expense in order to meet professors in the disciplines of their choice. Current minority and majority graduate students can be enlisted to participate in recruitment programs.

- *Identify colleges at which recruitment of minorities would be most productive and efficient.* Consider targeting historically black institutions or institutions with large numbers of minority students. The Hispanic Association of Colleges and Universities (HACU) is a national association that promotes educational opportunities for Hispanics at colleges and universities with significant Hispanic enrollments. Specific agreements with minority colleges can expand the pool and ease the admission process to graduate and professional programs. Such agreements may be focused on specific disciplines in which minority students are underrepresented.

Successful institutions build relationships with faculty, administrators, and students at these institutions, work on joint proposals to promote graduate studies and develop effective transition programs to bridge the gap between graduate and undergraduate education.

- *Encourage other joint ventures with minority institutions.* For example, many minority institutions have faculty members with master's degrees who are interested in pursuing doctoral work. They may be willing to share in the fellowship support of these faculty to study for the doctorate.

- *Develop effective recruitment materials aimed at minority undergraduates.* These materials might include brochures and other materials that are specific to departments and programs as well as the institution as a whole.

- *Advertise graduate and professional programs in national publications that minority undergraduates read* (e.g., *The Black Collegian, the Journal of National Association of Bilingual Education Journal, Black Issues in Higher Education, La Red, Essence, Ebony*).

- *Provide summer school research activities or assistantships at the graduate school for the sophomore, junior, and senior year.* Such efforts provide a bridge to graduate school and an incentive to pursue graduate education. Similar programs can be developed with minority schools with master's programs to guide students to the university's doctoral programs.

Admissions

The recruitment of minorities does not assure admission. Traditional selection criteria can work against minority students, excluding some with real potential who do not conform to the conventional profile of graduate or professional students. The following recommendations are derived from the experiences of institutions that have been successful in admitting minority graduate and professional students:

- *Use qualifying examinations judiciously.* Scores on the Graduate Record Examination (GRE), the Law School Admissions Test (LSAT), or the Medical College Admissions Test (MCAT) are commonly used as an admissions criterion, but their prediction of success in graduate and professional schools is uncertain. An approach to determining the usefulness of these tests as an admission criterion is to conduct studies to relate test scores to minority student achievement at the institution or department.

The GRE is not a universal requirement among graduate schools, and, even within a given university, it may not be required by all departments. Some departments require the score, but do not use it for admission. Some use it only for awarding financial aid. Because some minority students score low on these qualifying examinations, they assume this is an indication that they will not be successful in graduate school, and opt for other careers. Students should know how scores will be used and why the institution thinks a particular battery of tests is useful in determining eligibility.

The success of the graduate students participating in the McKnight Black Doctoral Fellowship Program (see description below) has documented success of recruiting some individuals who do not have high GRE scores but who have been highly successful in graduate study.

- *Use additional evaluative criteria such as interviews, professors' recommendations, autobiographical statements, and, of course, grade point averages.* Multiple sources of evidence will inevitably give a fuller picture of a student's achievements and potential.

- *Give undergraduate transcripts significant weight as an admission criterion.* Transcripts reliably measure students' ability to learn, as well as recording their previous coursework. Transcripts enable institutions to analyze academic strengths and weaknesses that are not revealed by the GPA and thus give a clearer picture of the person's potential for graduate work in a particular field of study.

It is important not to dismiss or devalue an institution simply because it is not well known or high in the institutional "pecking order." Doing so can deny admission to promising students. It is helpful to learn the standards of a student's college, the curriculum, and the professors.

- **■ *Be aware of possible bias in evaluating credentials of minority students.*** Subtle and often unconscious bias may negatively influence the evaluation of minority students. Subtle criteria that bear only marginal relevance to eventual graduate school performance may influence an individual's appraisal. For example, if interviews are used, speech and mannerisms can negatively influence the evaluation. Letters of recommendation, if written by unknown referees, or if from unknown institutions, may be devalued. Because of their backgrounds and cultural values, some minority students may be excessively modest in autobiographical statements, or not realize the need to promote themselves.

Recommendations are always a tricky issue. Some individuals may be reluctant to be at all critical of either minority or majority students. There are many reasons for this reluctance, and persons of good will may be especially unwilling to be critical of any student, especially minority students, for fear of jeopardizing their chances. The whole process, then, can lose credibility, and minority students may pay a heavier price.

- **■ *Consider using conditional admission procedures.*** Borderline but promising students might need some prerequisite courses, or they may have scored low on the GRE, LCAT, or MCAT, but achieved an acceptable undergraduate grade point average. Conditional admission allows the school to "bet" on the dedication and motivation of the student.

- **■ *Assist minority applicants in admission procedures.*** Institutions often do not take an active role in preparing students for the graduate and professional school admissions process. Some applicants will need guidance in preparing autobiographical statements and other parts of the application forms to ensure that they conform to the expectations and norms of the graduate institutions, and do not, for example, include irrelevant information. Graduate and professional school faculty members can work directly with prospective students or with undergraduate faculty to help their students understand the kinds of information that carry weight in the admissions process, including motivation for graduate study, academic experience, special experiences such as collaboration on research projects and outstanding term papers, and research-related travel or job experience.

Retention: Maximizing Success

A system of intellectual enrichment and student support helps meet the unique needs and concerns of minority students, and accustoms them to graduate and professional education. The "trial by fire" ethos of many graduate and professional schools may be especially intimidating to minority students, and special support from peers and faculty may be essential in helping them adjust to a difficult academic and social environment.

- *Support discipline-based minority student interest groups, such as blacks in psychology, or Hispanics in engineering.* These interest groups help graduate students develop a peer support network, and, additionally, link them to other minority groups on campus, to similar groups on other campuses, and to professional groups that can help increase minority graduate students' success.

- *Create academic support mechanisms.* Initiate help such as tutorial support in specialized subjects, computer lab assistance, and consultation on research methods. Support structures can also help students with housing, financial aid counseling, personal contacts for professional support, and job placement. Awards for leadership and for maintenance of high grade point averages are helpful incentives for all graduate students, but can be especially important to minority students.

- *Help students by reducing course loads when they need time to catch up with their peers. Any* student having trouble adjusting to graduate or professional school, or who is experiencing academic difficulties after the first semester or two, may be helped by reducing his or her course load, and hence lessening the stress. Minority students, who often experience greater adjustment problems than their white counterparts, may especially benefit from this practice if it is carried out in a nonpunitive manner.

- ***Promote programs that recognize distinctive cultural heritages.*** On all campuses, for undergraduate and graduate students, the issue of minorities in the intellectual and cultural life of the institution is central to the campus climate. Programs sponsored by various departments that feature minority speakers, or that deal with topics recognizing the contributions of minorities, send positive messages to minority students about their role on campus, and to majority students and faculty about outstanding minority scholars.

- ***Create a system of faculty mentors.*** Ideally, the faculty member serving as the student's advisor would also be a mentor to that student, regardless of racial background. Given the dearth of minority faculty members, white professors must assume the mentoring role for their minority graduate students. It is important to help faculty members understand the role of a mentor and to point out special areas of concern in mentoring minority students.

- ***Provide training to white faculty to help them become more understanding of minority student needs.*** Majority faculty may not be aware of behaviors in the classroom that can be negative or insulting to minority students. Workshops can be very useful to surface these issues and assist faculty in understanding the needs of minority students as well as their own values and behaviors.

- ***Encourage faculty members to become aware of the new issues in their disciplines that focus specifically on minority issues and concerns.*** Majority faculty may not automatically value or encourage minority-oriented research, and thereby discourage minority graduate and professional students from pursuing such issues or devalue their efforts when they do. Brown-bag lunches and other informal gatherings are good ways to get the conversations started.

- ***Help minority students understand how the graduate and professional school system works.*** Through meetings, mentoring, and workshops with faculty and peers, minority graduate and professional school students can be helped to understand that survival in graduate school requires more than the will to succeed. These sessions can stress the importance of relationships with faculty, the cultural norms of the institution and the department, as well as resources they can tap into to help them in this environment. Minority graduate students may also benefit from assistance in developing ties with graduate student clubs, student study groups, and campus chapters of national organizations such as Phi Delta Kappa.

- **Develop financial incentives for departments.** While the good will and enthusiasm of the faculty is integral to increasing minority access, incentives are also essential. Increased minority fellowship funds or graduate assistantships can be tied to the number of minorities recruited and graduated. Also, one criterion for awarding university-funded research seed grants could be a well-formulated plan to employ minorities on the project. Another incentive is a reduction in university overhead charged to extramural funds if minority graduate students are supported. An annual affirmative action grants competition can be used to encourage departments to do more. An annual affirmative action awards program can call attention to the importance of recruiting and retaining minority graduate students and affirm the institution's commitment to this goal.

Financial Aid

Financial support for graduate and professional school students is often tied to grade point average and qualifying exam scores rather than need. Yet minority graduate students are often the most needy. Therefore, need-based assistance is a primary requirement for the support of minority students. Here are some useful strategies:

- **Provide minority students with financial support packages that are adequate and guaranteed through the students' graduate careers, provided students make satisfactory academic progress.**

- **Award assistantships that complement studies.** Research, teaching, and administrative assistantships place students in close contact with professors, providing the potential for mentor relationships and informal learning. When seeking external funding, faculty can be encouraged to include assistantships for minority students in the proposal.

- **Ensure that sufficient scholarships are available for qualified minority students.**

- *Ensure that minority teaching fellows and research assistants are in the mainstream of academic and social activities of the department, including sharing graduate offices, working on research projects, attending informal social occasions.* Social isolation affects the ability of minority students to learn the academic culture; without that knowledge it is difficult to succeed.

- *Seek financial arrangements with external sources.* It is extremely helpful to develop consortial relationships with private industries and other universities in order to increase financial assistance. Examples include the CIC Minorities Fellowships Program, GEM and COGME (described in the Programs and Practices section at the end of this chapter).

- *Support students needing part-time work.* Minority student will generally have greater need for financial assistance than majority students. Minority students should be encouraged to apply for college work-study funds through graduate school financial aid officers. All students benefit from work opportunities that complement and reinforce their studies. A clearinghouse of part-time employment outside the university can also be useful to needy students.

- *Offer financial aid packages that provide more grants than loans.* Loan burdens are a disincentive for minority students to continue in graduate school. To the extent possible, financial aid packages for needy minority students should have a high proportion of grants and a low proportion of loans and work.

- *Assist minority students with loans.* While loans are the least desirable form of financial assistance for needy students, some indebtedness is often inevitable. Assistance in identifying sources of loans and in completing the paperwork for all aid is very helpful. A loan fund for student emergencies is also useful.

CHECKLIST

Many of the strategies listed below will be useful to your institution; others will not. Apply the following questions to each item on the checklist to determine its usefulness:

- If the answer is *yes,* is the strategy or policy effective? How do you assess how well it is working? Are outcome data available?

- If the answer is *no,* would such an approach be useful? How high a priority would you place on developing such a policy or strategy?

Expanding the Pool

Suggested reviewers: graduate and professional school faculty and staff, department heads, graduate students.

1. Are efforts made to cultivate the interest of minority undergraduates at the institution in pursuing graduate and professional education?

2. Are relationships developed with possible feeder institutions?

3. Are potential graduate and professional school students made aware of the entry requirements for graduate study?

4. Are special opportunities for research under the guidance of graduate students and faculty made available to prospective minority students?

5. Are local businesses and other employers aware of opportunities for graduate and professional study for their employees? Have special programs been developed to meet their needs?

Recruitment

Suggested reviewers: admissions personnel, graduate and professional school administrators, department heads, faculty.

1. Does the faculty have networks with institutions that have large numbers of minority students?

2. Are working adults recruited for graduate and professional programs? Are the programs sufficiently flexible to accommodate their needs?

3. Do prospective minority graduate and professional school students have opportunities to visit the campus and meet with faculty and students?

Admissions

Suggested reviewers: same as above.

1. Are admissions criteria reviewed to ensure that they do not discriminate against minority students?

2. Is help available to minority students in the application process?

3. If conditional admission is offered to minority students, is it reinforced by academic and financial counseling that will increase their chances of success?

Retention

Suggested reviewers: graduate and professional school administrators, department heads, faculty, students.

1. Is help available to students experiencing academic difficulty? Are steps taken to ensure that students requesting help are not stigmatized?

2. Are fellowships and assistantships available to minority students that reinforce the learning process?

3. Do majority and minority faculty take an active role in mentoring minority graduate students? Is assistance given to faculty in mentoring?

4. Does the curriculum and co-curriculum recognize distinctive cultural heritages and their contribution to various fields?

5. Are white faculty trained to understand the special needs of minority students?

6. Are faculty encouraged to keep up with research areas currently being explored by many minority students and faculty? rewarded for it?

Financial Aid

Suggested reviewers: financial aid personnel, graduate deans, department heads.

1. Do financial aid packages contain sufficient grants to avoid excessive loan burdens for poor minority students?

2. Is sufficient financial aid available to cover the costs of the minority student's entire graduate career, or does it drop off after the first year or two?

3. Is there sufficient need-based financial aid available for minority students?

PROGRAMS AND PRACTICES

Expanding the Pool

Association for Education in Journalism, New York University, Summer Internship for Minorities in Journalism. Begun in 1970, this summer program prepares minority students

for careers in the media as well as increases the number of
minorities in the industry. The 10-week program for juniors
or seniors going on to graduate school includes placement in
a full-time (35 hours per week) paid internship with participating companies, and enrollment in a two-credit course,
which is designed to help students develop writing, editing,
research, and interviewing skills.
CONTACT: *Sidique A. Wai, Program Coordinator, (212)
998-1212.*

**Summer Fellowship Program for Minority Premedical Stu-
dents, Cornell University Medical School.** This seven-week
summer program was developed in 1969 to enable premedical college students to get a preliminary look at medical
school life and to give participants deeper insights into their
future careers and into the wide range of options that exist
for minority physicians. Students spend four days per week
in research under the supervision of a faculty member. The
remaining day is spent in seminars on cardiovascular physi-
ology, public health topics, and careers in medicine. Students
receive a $120 a week stipend to cover living costs, and are
house in the medical students' dormitory. An evaluation of
the program is available.
CONTACT: *Bruce L. Ballard, M.D., Associate Dean, (212)
472-5668.*

**The Mellon/Ford Summer Minority Research Exchange Pro-
gram.** Begun in 1985, the program provides summer research
internships in engineering and the biological, physical, and
social sciences for sophomores and juniors enrolled at Cornell,
Princeton, Stanford, the University of California–Berkeley, the
University of California–Los Angeles, and Yale. The goal is to
increase the number of American ethnic-minority students who
enter Ph.D. programs preparatory to pursuing careers in university teaching and research. Internships are offered on a competitive basis; each intern is hosted by one of the six universities
for an eight-week period. All research, under individual faculty
sponsorship, is substantive and requires the full-time commitment of the student. Weekly meetings or seminars are held
with the expectation that the student will be able to discuss the
research design and progress. A final abstract is required with
an oral presentation at the end of the eight-week session. The
program is coordinated by Cornell University.

CONTACT: *Eleanor Cox, Assistant Dean of the Graduate School, Cornell University. (607) 255-5235.*

Black Scholars Program, Woodrow Wilson National Fellowship Foundation. In 1987, the Woodrow Wilson National Fellowship Foundation initiated the Black Scholars Program to contribute to increasing the number of black faculty. Because large numbers of black students are concentrated in the historically black institutions, seven of these were chosen to participate in the program. Each hosted a prominent black scholar who spent a week on campus, encouraging outstanding students to consider entering graduate study as preparation for careers as scholars and teachers. While on campus, the scholars meet with classes and bring to students and faculty the latest scholarship in their fields. In addition, they meet with administrators to encourage the creation of honors programs, with students and teachers in these programs where they exist, and with the career development officers to ensure that the latest information on graduate school admissions and fellowships is available. Most important, they also meet with individual students to discuss careers in academe. The program will be expanded to include additional institutions in 1988–89.
CONTACT: *Judith Pinch, Program Officer, (609) 924-4666.*

Summer Institute In Health Related Professions, Indiana University, Bloomington. Initiated in 1973, the Institute exposes minority, disadvantaged, and low-income undergraduate students from any accredited institution to the many career opportunities in the health field. The students spend six weeks on campus attending lectures, visiting area hospitals, participating in laboratory exercises, and studying in the various science disciplines. The program also provides individual counseling in academic and career planning throughout the six weeks. Four hours of undergraduate credit at Indiana University are awarded for successful completion. Sponsors of the institute include the School of Optometry, Indiana University, and the Department of Health and Human Services.
CONTACT: *Dr. Edwin Marshall, Director, (812) 335-4475.*

Access Internally for Minorities (AIM), Purdue University. Begun in 1981, the *Summer Research Opportunities Pro-*

gram, aims to increase the number of minority students in graduate school in fields where they are underrepresented. It is currently aimed at students from Purdue and several historically black colleges. There are three complementary components. The primary one involves minority sophomores and juniors in research and scholarly activities with faculty mentors. This in-depth research experience, working one-on-one with a faculty member, results in significant student learning and in the development of a strong student/faculty relationship. The second component, the campus-based activities, broadens the student's view of graduate education and research and creates an *esprit de corps* among the participants. Campus workshops inform students about graduate admission procedures, financial aid opportunities, test-taking skills, preparing presentations, and university resources. The seminars, conducted by faculty and graduate students, expose the undergraduates to a wide range of research. Informal social gatherings provide a relaxed setting for students and faculty to exchange ideas and share experiences. At the end of the summer, a symposium is held on campus during which students present research findings.
CONTACT: *Dwight Lewis, Minority Affairs Assistant, (317) 494-3232.*

Pre-Law Institute, American Indian Law Center, Inc. This eight-week summer institute at the University of New Mexico is aimed at Native American students who have applied to law school and taken the LSAT. The program provides an introduction to the study of law. Courses and materials are provided without charge and a small living stipend is provided. Eligible candidates must provide proof of membership in a federally recognized tribe, a certificate of Degree of Indian Blood, an undergraduate transcript, and a copy of the LSAT/LSDAS report indicating the applicant's LSAT score.
CONTACT: *Barbara Alvarez, (505) 277-5462.*

Early Identification Program, University of Washington. This program is designed to identify talented minority undergraduates and encourage them to pursue graduate degrees. Students are selected after their freshman year, and must have a cumulative GPA of 3.2 or above. Among the program's features are student visits to industries and organizations, academic advising and counseling, instructional enhancement labs, instructional assistance, faculty mentoring programs, summer research internships, test preparation classes, and

assistance in the application process to graduate school. It operates as a smaller unit within the university and provides a "home base." Outcome data are available.
CONTACT: *Norihiko Mihara, Assistant Vice President, (206) 543-6598.*

The Ohio State University Graduate School Minority Programs. Ohio State has a number of programs in place to identify and recruit minority graduate students. Among them are:

- **Minority Name Exchange Programs.** The graduate school participates in several name exchange programs: the GRE minority Locator Service, the CIC Name Exchange, and the National Name Exchange. In the National Name Exchange Program and in the CIC Name Exchange Program, each university supplies the other participating universities with information regarding minority juniors and seniors interested in attending graduate school. These lists are distributed by the graduate school to departments and programs. Each identified student is sent appropriate literature and invited to apply to Ohio State.

- **Graduate School Recruitment Grant Program.** A competition open to all graduate programs for funds to support departmental recruitment of graduate students is held each year. One area of emphasis is the recruitment of minority students. To date 60 academic departments have received one or more awards of up to $5,000 to assist in the recruitment of minority students.

- **Campus Visitation Program.** This program provides travel funds for campus visits by nominees for fellowships.

- **Graduate and Professional Schools Visitation Days.** This program brings to campus annually approximately 300 minority students from 60 historically black institutions and 10 institutions with large Hispanic enrollments.

- **Recruitment Workshops.** Workshops on recruitment strategies are held for representatives of graduate programs, including special emphasis on recruitment of minority students.

- **Summer Research Opportunities Program.** Undergraduate minority students are selected in a competition to work with a faculty mentor on a research project during a summer quarter following their sophomore or junior year. In 1987-88, 56 awards were made.

CONTACT: *Roy A. Koenigsknecht, Dean of the Graduate School, (614) 292-6031.*

Retention: Maximizing Success

Medical Education Support Project (MESP), Michigan State University Program. Initiated in 1984, this project aims to identify and select disadvantaged students to attend medical school. It provides a summer enrichment program and on-going admissions support activities. Also, a summer orientation and retention program help strengthen the skills necessary for success in medical school. Along with providing academic and personal support services, the program provides a review program to assist the students in preparing for the National Board of Medical Examiners Examination. Thus, the program involves recruitment, facilitating entry, admissions, and retention of minority medical students.

CONTACT: *Dr. Wanda Lipscomb, Director, (517) 353-5440.*

Graduate Research Mentorship Program (GRMP), University of California–Santa Barbara. Begun in 1983, GRMP is a three-tier, learner-centered research mentorship program involving undergraduate and graduate research assistants and faculty members. Undergraduates are mentored by graduate research students, and the faculty researcher mentors both graduate and undergraduate project participants. The aim of the program is to introduce minority undergraduates to the excitement and importance of academic research, and to encourage them to attend graduate school and consider academic research as a career option. In addition, participating graduate students complete their degrees considerably faster than students not involved in mentorship, publish and present professional papers earlier, and are generally better prepared to enter the job market. Outcome data are available.

CONTACT: *Dr. Richard Duran, (805) 961-4489.*

Board of Regents (BOR) Summer Program, University of Florida. The BOR Summer Program has prepared new black graduate students for graduate studies at the University of Florida since 1978. The program is designed to increase black student enrollment and retention rates. Some of the major objectives of the BOR program include: familiarizing students with academic programs and policies, informing students about support services available for them, helping

students adjust to the school's academic and social environments, and introducing students to the black faculty, staff, and students. The program provides incoming black graduate students with information about what skills are needed to succeed in their pursuit of a graduate degree. An evaluation of the program is available.
CONTACT: *Dr. Roderick J. McDavis, Associate Dean for Graduate Studies, (904) 392-5868.*

Financial Aid

Institutional programs

Graduate Dean's Fellowships, Southern Illinois University, Carbondale. Since 1968, these fellowships have been offered to students who show promise of success in graduate studies even though their previous academic achievements may have been hindered because they are minorities, of low socioeconomic status, or women. The awards are usually made to students who are well qualified by the usual indicators, such as undergraduate grade point averages and GRE or MAT scores, but whose disadvantaged status has meant that their records are not impressive enough for them to have received openly competitive fellowship awards.
CONTACT: *Karen Jennings, Graduate School, (618) 536-7791.*

Minority Fellowships, The Ohio State University. The graduate school offers a number of fellowships to new minority students in their first year of graduate studies who are pursuing either a master's or Ph.D. degree. One-year Minority Fellowships and Multiple-Year Minority Fellowships are offered. Among the fellowships are Special University Fellowships, awarded to students who need to complete undergraduate prerequisites to prepare for graduate work, who are graduates of little-known institutions, or who have low scores on qualifying examinations.
CONTACT: *Roy A. Koenigsknecht, Dean of the Graduate School, (614) 292-6031.*

Consortium programs

Committee on Institutional Cooperation (CIC) Minorities Fellowships Program. The CIC Minorities Fellowships Program awards 35 four-year fellowships to minority students seeking doctorates in a wide variety of fields in the social sciences and humanities. The fellowships provide full tuition and an

annual stipend of at least $8,000. Sponsored by the Committee on Institutional Cooperation (CIC), the academic consortium of the Big Ten universities, and the University of Chicago, the fellowships may be used at any one of the 11 CIC universities to which recipients have been admitted. In operation since 1978, the CIC Minorities Fellowships Program has become the model on which other minorities fellowship programs are based. To date, over 400 students from all sections of the country have received CIC fellowships to support their graduate studies at CIC universities. Participating institutions are: the University of Chicago, the University of Illinois, the University of Iowa, Indiana University, the University of Michigan, Michigan State University, the University of Minnesota, Northwestern University, Ohio State University, Purdue University, and the University of Wisconsin–Madison. Major funding for the program comes from the Lilly Endowment, Inc. and the Andrew W. Mellon Foundation.
CONTACT: *CIC Minorities Fellowship Program, 1-800-457-4420.*

Consortium for Graduate Study in Management (CGSM).
The Consortium for Graduate Study in Management is a nine-university alliance to assist minorities in preparing for managerial positions in business. Participating schools are Indiana University, University of Michigan, New York University, the University of North Carolina at Chapel Hill, the University of Rochester, the University of Southern California, the University of Texas–Austin, Washington University, and the University of Wisconsin. The Consortium allows candidates to apply for admission and fellowship consideration at any four of the nine member schools. Each person who qualifies for admission then competes for a consortium fellowship of full tuition and fees plus $5,000 stipend to one of the member universities to pursue an MBA degree. Fellowship winners are provided with a comprehensive orientation program during the summer prior to matriculation. The program has supported 1,300 students in 22 years.
CONTACT: *Brent E. Johnson, Director for Marketing and Recruiting, (314) 889-5614.*

National Consortium for Graduate Degrees for Minorities in Engineering, Inc. (GEM). GEM is a consortium consisting of 54 universities and 60 co-sponsoring industrial organizations. Its primary efforts are geared towards increasing the number of ethnic minorities with a master's degree in engineering and to help bring minorities into leadership positions in the engineering profession. Competitive fellowships which cover tuition costs and a $5,000 stipend per academic year are provided to promising minority students in engineering at the participating universities. During the summers before and between graduate study, the fellows are provided engineering-related employment by one of the participating industrial members. The program also is heavily engaged in recruitment, with numerous conferences and college visits throughout the country to encourage more minorities to enter graduate engineering programs.

CONTACT: *Dr. Howard G. Adams, Executive Director, (219) 239-7183.*

State programs

New Jersey Minority Academic Career Program (MAC). In operation for three years, MAC is designed to increase the presence of underrepresented minority group members in New Jersey institutions. Awards are available to support minority students pursuing doctoral degrees at one of eight New Jersey Institutions: Drew University, Fairleigh Dickinson University, New Jersey Institute of Technology, Princeton University, Rutgers University, Seton Hall University, Stevens Institute of Technology and the University of Medicine and Dentistry of New Jersey. The program fellow must be awarded an annual stipend of at least $5,000 from the doctoral institution and may apply for loans of up to $10,000 per year during as many as four years through the Minority Academic Career Program. The loans are interest-free so long as the recipient is enrolled in the program or is performing approved redemption service at a New Jersey college. One-quarter of the loan value will be canceled for each full year of qualified employment service following completion of the program.

CONTACT: *New Jersey Department of Higher Education, (609) 292-5833.*

The California State University Forgivable Loan/Doctoral Incentive Program. Launched a year ago, this three-year pilot program is designed to increase the sex and racial/ethnic diversity of faculty in selected academic fields in the California

State University (CSU) campuses. Student loans of up to $30,000 over three years are to be forgiven if the student gains a full-time position at a CSU institution. Students must be sponsored by CSU faculty who assist in their professional development and serve as mentors. Upon completion of their doctorates, if the students become full-time faculty members in CSU, their loans will be forgiven at the rate of 20 percent per year for five years. Sixty awards were made in 1987; 40 more students will be funded in the 1988–89 academic year. The program is open to new or continuing full-time students in doctoral programs at accredited California universities.
CONTACT: *Tim T. L. Dong, State University Dean, Affirmative Action, (213) 590-5603.*

Black Doctoral Fellowships, Florida Endowment Fund (formerly the McKnight Black Doctoral Fellowship Program). This program aims to increase the number of qualified black faculty in Florida. Some 25 fellowships are awarded each year for doctoral study at Florida public or private institutions in the arts and sciences, business, and engineering. Fellowships are awarded for a three-year period, covering up to $5,000 tuition and fees and a $11,000 annual stipend. To date, 92 fellowships have been awarded. The program was initiated with a $10 million challenge grant to the governor of Florida from the McKnight Foundation, to be matched by the state legislature.
CONTACT: *Israel Tribble, Jr., President, Florida Endowment Fund for Higher Education, (813) 221-2772.*

Illinois Consortium Educational Opportunity Program (ICEOP) Award. Created in 1985, ICEOP provides financial assistance for minority graduate students in Illinois public and private institutions. Its purpose is to increase the number of minority faculty and staff in Illinois colleges, universities, and educational agencies. The annual appropriation is made to the Board of Higher Education for allocation to awardees selected by a consortium board. Institutions serve as fiscal agents and pay monthly stipends to awardees. Each award provides up to $10,000 annually. Participants in doctoral programs are eligible to receive awards for up to four years; those in master's or professional programs may receive awards for up to two years. An award recipient must agree to accept a full-time teaching or nonteaching position with an Illinois postsecondary institution or an Illinois education

board or agency for a period equal to the number of years that awards were received. Applicants must be residents of Illinois and demonstrate financial need. Students apply directly to the ICEOP participating institution that they plan to attend.
CONTACT: *Graduate Schools of Illinois institutions.*

National programs

Minority Graduate Fellowships, National Science Foundation. Designed to increase the number of minority scientists and engineers, the NSF minority fellowships are awarded to members of traditionally underrepresented ethnic minority groups who have demonstrated an ability and aptitude for advanced study in the fields of science or engineering. The recipients are expected to pursue a master's or doctoral degree in the field of science, mathematics, or engineering.
CONTACT: *Fellowship Office, National Research Council, (202) 334-2872.*

Patricia Roberts Harris Fellowships Programs (formerly Graduate and Professional Study Fellowships Program [GPOP]). This program provides grants to institutions of higher education to support fellowships for graduate and professional study to students who demonstrate financial need and who are predominantly from groups that are traditionally underrepresented in graduate and professional study areas.
CONTACT: *Division of Higher Education Incentive Programs, Office of Postsecondary Education, Department of Education, (202) 732-4395.*

5

FACULTY

A diverse faculty is essential to a pluralistic campus. Faculty create the curriculum and determine the quality of the experience in every classroom. They serve as teachers, mentors, advisors, and role models. In a word, faculty are the core of the institution. Without the contributions of minority individuals, no faculty or institution can be complete.

THE CURRENT SITUATION

Less than 11 percent of faculty members are minority group members. As the table below indicates, between 1977 and 1985, the number of black faculty barely increased; their share of all faculty positions dropped from 4.4 percent to 4.2 percent. These figures represent *all* black faculty; black representation on faculties in predominantly white institutions is only 1.8 percent. Representation of Hispanics and American Indians in the faculty ranks remains low, in spite of modest overall gains in the last decade. The number of Hispanic faculty rose by over 1,000 between 1977 and 1983, increasing slightly as a proportion of all faculty members from 1.5 percent to 1.7 percent. However, the number of Hispanic faculty declined between 1983 and 1985. Only the number of Asians increased substantially; there were 7,000 more Asian faculty in 1985 than in 1977, and their proportion of all faculty grew from 2.7 percent to 4.1 percent.

As the discussion in Chapter 4 indicated, the lack of progress in improving minority representation among the faculty is largely a function of the small pool of minority doctorate holders. In 1981, 2,728 doctorates were awarded to minority students; that number remained nearly level in 1987, at

2,890. The number of blacks receiving doctorates during this period actually fell by over 300, from 1,265 to 904 in 1987.

Further compounding the problem is the concentration of minority group members in certain fields. Blacks are concentrated in the fields of education and the social sciences; Hispanics follow similar, but not as dramatic, patterns.

Also, minority faculty are less likely to hold tenure than majority faculty. In 1985 (according to a 1988 report of the Minority Graduate Education Project by Shirley Vining Brown), 62 percent of the black faculty in four-year colleges, 66 percent of the Hispanic faculty, and 65 percent of the Asian faculty were tenured, compared with 71 percent of all faculty. However, minority faculty were more likely than whites to be in tenure-track positions.

The study also showed that the proportion of black doctorate holders choosing academic careers has declined over the past 10 years: in 1975, more than two-thirds of the black Ph.D. recipients planned to pursue academic employment, compared with slightly under one-half in 1986. Since these proportions are based on a declining number of blacks earning doctorates, the problem is further exacerbated. The proportion of white graduate students planning to enter academe also fell from 60 to 48 percent during that period—but the

Table 3: Full-time Faculty by Race/Ethnicity

	1977		1983		1985	
	Number	Percentage	Number	Percentage	Number	Percentage
Total	449,210	100.0	473,787	100.0	478,267	100.0
White	409,974	91.3	428,977	90.5	429,154	89.7
Black	19,674	4.4	18,827	4.0	19,850	4.2
Hispanic	6,605	1.5	8,311	1.8	7,983	1.7
Asian/ Pacific Islander	11,917	2.7	16,398	3.5	19,421	4.1
American Indian	1,040	0.2	1,274	0.3	1,855	0.4

Source: *Minorities in Higher Education: Fifth Annual Status Report.* Washington D.C.: American Council on Education, 1986, p. 35 and 1985 Equal Employment Opportunity Commission, EEO-6 Detail Summary report, NCES unpublished tabulations.

larger size of the pool of white doctorate holders caused faculty shortages in only a few fields.

STRATEGIES

As the small numbers of minority doctorate and master's holders indicate, the underrepresentation of minorities is largely, but not entirely, a supply problem. Thus, strategies to recruit and retain minority faculty must be intimately tied to efforts to recruit undergraduate and graduate students.

But increasing the numbers in the pipeline is not the only strategy and represents a long-term effort. A second approach is to look outside the traditional ranks of new Ph.D.s—to business, industry and government—and to explore innovative approaches such as faculty exchanges with historically black institutions or visiting appointments.

A third strategy is to be sure that the search process covers the entire pool. While there is certainly a danger of institutions competing for a small pool of minority Ph.D.s, especially for the academic stars, a thorough and aggressive search may yield surprising results. Also, insisting on results and holding department chairs and academic administrators accountable for improving minority participation may also turn up minority candidates who might otherwise be missed.

Finally, the job of increasing the number of minority faculty does not end with the recruitment process. Ensuring their success through promotion and tenure is a vital component of the effort.

Many of the strategies in this chapter were described in "The University of California in the Twenty-First Century: Successful Approaches to Faculty Diversity" (see under "Resources" at the end of this chapter). In its plan to enhance faculty diversity, the study group identified important general principles that undergird any specific recommended strategies to recruit minority and women faculty. The plan specifies that the University of California will:

- ***Examine ways in which quality can be innovatively pursued,*** to enable departments to increase the number of women and minority faculty they hire.

- *Encourage departments to use new methods to discover a more diverse range of scholars,* while maintaining standards of excellence.

- *Encourage departments not only to look for excellence when they are ready to hire, but to create an environment in which students, visitors, and junior faculty can grow and excel.*

- *Create an environment that supports scholarly production* and that positively affects the "quality of life" of scholars to enhance their output.

- *Commit itself to a "pipeline approach,"* providing support at key points, and recognizing the importance of integrating all the parts to produce a total effect that is greater than the sum of its parts.

- *Commit itself to short-term strategies* as well as the long-term pipeline approach.

These general principles are developed more concretely in the strategies outlined below.

Expanding the Pool

Expanding the pool of potential minority faculty should, of course, include long-term efforts to increase the numbers of minority graduate students. But it should also include efforts to go beyond the traditional pool of minority faculty at predominantly white institutions or new Ph.D.s, as illustrated by the following strategies:

- *Implement short-term appointments or exchanges of minority faculty from HBCUs.* These approaches provide role models, establish contacts with other universities, and assist in future recruiting efforts.

- *Seek out individuals who are currently outside of academe: in corporations, the military, or the government.* Short-term faculty appointments are an option, as well as a longer commitment through a career change. Faculty can use their contacts in the community and in the profession to develop a pool of such individuals to tap when a position is available.

- *Create research jobs or part-time teaching positions for minority individuals.* This "foot in the door" provides an active minority presence in the department as well as a pool to consider to future positions.

■ *Create postdoctoral fellowships as an enticement to minorities for permanent faculty positions.*

■ *Hire minority individuals who have completed all Ph.D. requirements but their dissertations (ABDs) and provide a follow-up program of faculty development that permits the completion of the doctoral degree.*

■ *Create a visiting scholars program or distinguished lecturer series.* This can expose students and faculty to new perspectives and scholarship, enriching the academic environment for all.

Preparation

When a vacancy occurs, it is natural for a department to think of the new person in terms of the expertise of the departing one, or of the programmatic needs immediately identified as central to the department's mission. A vacancy can be an occasion for a department to rethink its programmatic needs and tie them directly to enhancing diversity among the faculty. Thus, departments are well advised to:

■ *Take time for planning to reconsider the programmatic needs and how these needs can be linked to recruiting minority faculty.*

■ *Write position descriptions to ensure that they attract the widest possible range of candidates.* Broad definitions of scholarly areas of interest will be more likely to attract scholars with specialties in minority or third world issues or who have the flexibility to do research and teach in a number of related areas.

■ *Define "quality," and air possible biases.* Discuss standards of excellence in teaching, research, and service. What are realistic expectations? How might minority candidates look "different" but also "excellent"? Is there a bias, spoken or unspoken, against individuals from lesser-known institutions or from HBCUs? Is scholarship on minority issues or in minority journals consciously or unconsciously devalued by majority faculty? What can a minority faculty person contribute to the department that a majority individual cannot?

■ *Have the affirmative action officer brief the search committee on proper procedures before the search begins.*

Roles and Responsibilities

Deans and academic vice presidents

Deans and vice presidents play a pivotal role in encouraging and supporting department chairs as they recruit and hire faculty. Academic officers can help department chairs in their efforts to recruit minority faculty by doing the following:

- Providing workshops or orientation sessions for department chairs. These should include training on how to conduct searches, how to identify a wide pool of candidates using nontraditional strategies, how to help minority faculty be successful, and so forth.

- Providing incentives to hire minority faculty through extra faculty slots or additional departmental monies.

- Setting specific institutional goals and delineating the role of departments in meeting those goals.

Department chairs

Department chairs can take the following actions:

- *Keep an up-to-date list of minority graduate students in the discipline; stay in touch with them.* At the Massachusetts Institute of Technology, for example, each department chair has such a list and maintains an active network with faculty at other institutions, with graduate students, and with postdoctoral students.

- *Take an active role in the recruiting process,* contacting fellow department chairs around the country.

- *Monitor the process* to ensure that an active search is being conducted and that search committee members are soliciting nominations and applications from a variety of sources.

- *Review all the dossiers of minority candidates personally.*

- *Ensure that qualified minority candidates are included in the final pool.*

The Search Process

Identifying candidates

The best search process is an active one. Advertising is only one step, perhaps the least effective. Successful search committees have found the following strategies to be helpful:

- *Involve the affirmative action officer at each step of the search process.* He or she should brief the search committee, review every minority applicant's resume, and, if possible, participate in the interviews.

- *Use their personal and professional networks to identify potential candidates—including professional associations and colleagues at other institutions.*

- *Telephone potential minority candidates and invite them to apply.*

- *Tap into existing relationships with HBCUs or consult with them for nominees.*

- *Use minority administrators, faculty, and support groups to assist them in identifying candidates.*

- *Search outside of academe, considering former faculty members or individuals with the potential to serve as faculty members.*

The interview process

As elaborated in the following chapter on administrators, the interview process is crucial. The approaches described below are simple, good practice; they are relevant to majority and minority candidates, but often more problematical and, therefore, more important to minority candidates.

The quality of life that a faculty member can expect, the relationship with colleagues, and the culture of an institution and the department all become clearer to a candidate when he or she is brought on campus. Issues to cover in the interview include:

- *Expectations for tenure.* It is important to discuss realistically and openly the standards of scholarly productivity, of teaching and research *with all candidates.* Since minority faculty so often feel the pull between the activities that are rewarded by tenure and those that are generally not, it is helpful to discuss these tensions outright. Committee service, for example, especially when there are few minorities to "go around" on committees, as well as heavier obligations to minority students as advisors and mentors, are often important and time-consuming parts of the minority faculty person's professional life. However, they detract from time for research. It is helpful to discuss strategies for minimizing these conflicts at the interview stage.

■ *Quality of life in the community.* Candidates will want to know about housing, schools, community activities, and the general atmosphere of the institution and the town with respect to minority individuals and families. It is helpful to have minority candidates talk with other minority members of the campus community. It is also important, however, that the department chair and fellow majority colleagues help with housing, schools, and community activities. This is the clearest indication that the candidate will be welcomed by all his or her colleagues.

■ *Spouse employment.* Often, lack of employment for a spouse may prevent a candidate from moving to an institution. While institutions cannot necessarily produce a job for the spouse, they can assist the spouse in finding a position. A formal institutional commitment to assistance makes a big difference. In the case of an academic couple, split appointments are sometimes an option. Also, sometimes it is helpful to delay the starting time of the appointment to meet candidates' personal needs.

Making an offer

The competition among institutions for minority faculty members is real. Certainly, colleges and universities have already experienced the forces of the marketplace with respect to faculty in high demand disciplines. Institutions must recognize the need to woo minority faculty to their institutions and provide attractive offers. Attractive offers (for any faculty member) may include the following:

■ *Above-market salaries.* As in fields with high demand, such as business or computer science, the scarcity of minority faculty may cause institutions to consider offering higher salaries than they would to a majority candidate. Institutions will want to weigh this strategy carefully.

■ *Housing subsidies.* In areas with high housing costs, a subsidy may make the offer more attractive.

■ *Support for research and professional meetings.*

■ *Provision for course loads that enable the person to meet tenure expectations.*

Retention and Professional Success

As with student recruitment, the task does not end once a faculty member is hired. As mentioned above, *all* junior faculty need to know what the expectations are before they are hired. Minority faculty have special burdens placed on them because they are so few. These expectations come from students, the community, and the institution. Unless institutions are prepared to recognize these contributions as being equally important as scholarship, tenure, and promotion criteria, ways must be found to lighten this load and ensure that minority faculty have the same opportunities for publication and professional growth as their majority counterparts. Some successful approaches to ensuring the success of junior faculty include:

- *Reducing teaching and committee loads in the first few years.*

- *Providing half-year sabbaticals in the third year.* A sabbatical at this point permits junior faculty to be sure that their research and publication are on solid ground well before the tenure review process begins.

- *Provide funds for research and opportunities to work with senior professors.* Junior faculty can benefit greatly from the sponsorship and mentorship of senior professors. Senior professors, usually white males, need to take an active role in working with their junior minority colleagues both in research and in advising them on how to navigate the tenure process.

- *Be sure that the tenure process does not disadvantage minority faculty members.* Faculty members who conduct research on minority issues and who publish in minority-focused journals may be disadvantaged in the tenure review process by their colleagues' lack of familiarity with these areas and publications, or by their devaluation of different scholarly endeavors.

- *Attend to the continuing professional development of junior faculty members.* The professional vitality of *all* faculty members is crucial to the well-being of any institution. Thus, a vigorous program of faculty development, encouraging new areas of research, improved teaching, and faculty leadership will benefit all. Institutions should ensure that minority faculty are well informed of opportunities and procedures for fellowships and grant support.

Of particular note is the importance of identifying minority faculty who show promise as academic administrators. Nominations to programs such as the ACE Fellows Program, HERS/Bryn Mawr Summer Institute for Women (described below), and the creation of on-campus programs provide important avenues of administrative development.

CHECKLIST

Consider the following items in light of the two questions used in other checklists:

- If the answer is *yes,* is the strategy effective? How do you assess how well it is working? What outcome data are available?

- If the answer is *no,* would such an approach be useful at your institution? How high a priority would you place on developing such a strategy or policy?

Expanding the Pool

Suggested reviewers: academic administrators, department chairs, faculty.

1. What measures have been taken to identify nontraditional sources of faculty, for example, exchanges or visiting appointments of faculty from HBCUs, visiting lectureships, persons in industry or government?

2. Do faculty and department chairs have active networks with majority institutions and HBCUs to identify future faculty members? How do they update and maintain these networks?

Recruiting

Suggested reviewers: academic administrators, department chairs, faculty.

1. Does the affirmative action officer play an active role in every stage of the search process?

2. Is information made available through workshops, orientation sessions, or printed materials to help search committees recruit widely and maximize their chances of recruiting minority faculty?

3. Are incentives provided to hire minority faculty?

4. Are efforts being made to recruit minority candidates actively? If so, which are the most effective?

5. Has the position description been written in such a way as to attract the widest possible range of candidates?

Screening

1. Are procedures in place to ensure that minority candidates are reviewed carefully, with an eye to being inclusive rather than exclusive?

2. Are steps taken to ensure that minority candidates are included in the final pool?

3. Have the screening criteria been reviewed to ensure that they are not working against minority candidates?

Interviews

1. Are expectations for tenure clearly articulated to the candidates?

2. Are minority candidates fully informed about factors affecting personal and family issues, including the housing, schools, the minority community within and outside the institution?

3. Do minority candidates have the opportunity to meet with minority faculty, administrators, students during the interview process?

Employment offers

1. Is the compensation package competitive, especially in fields where minority faculty are in high demand?

2. Is there adequate support for research, attendance at professional meetings, and other activities necessary for tenure and promotion?

Retention and Professional Success

1. Are teaching loads and committee assignments such that a junior faculty member will be able to meet the requirements for tenure?

2. Are funds for research available?

3. Are there opportunities for minority junior faculty to work with senior professors?

4. Are minority faculty members with leadership abilities identified and encouraged? Are they sponsored for campus and national leadership development programs and opportunities?

PROGRAMS AND PRACTICES

Recruitment

Minority Teaching Fellowship Program, Catonsville Community College. Catonsville Community College has developed a teaching assistantship for minority graduate students recruited from regional colleges and universities, as well as for individuals seeking a career change into teaching. The program aims to provide Catonville's students with diverse faculty, to infuse new approaches and techniques into current courses, to provide an additional mechanism for recruiting minority faculty members, and to provide an opportunity for members of minority groups to participate in a one-year program of professional development and training at the college. A faculty mentor is designated for each fellow, who is paid a full salary and benefits, serves on campus committees, teaches regular college classes, and can be considered for permanent faculty appointments when positions become available.
CONTACT: *Judy Snyder, Affirmative Action Officer, (301) 455-4294.*

Langston Hughes Visiting Professorship, University of Kansas. The purpose of this program is to provide a succession of visiting professors who are exemplary for the university as a whole, and especially for minority students and faculty. The visiting professor is appointed for one semester, and, whenever possible, he or she will have a joint appointment in African and African-American Studies, and will teach at least one course in African and African-American Studies. A faculty committee, drawn from a cross-section of the university, is responsible for recommending candidates for the professorship to the Vice Chancellor for Academic Affairs.
CONTACT: *Carol Prentice, Assistant to the Vice Chancellor for Academic Affairs, (913) 864-4455.* (See also Financial Aid section, under *Programs and Practices,* in Chapter 5.)

Professional Development for Junior Faculty

Junior Faculty Development Fellowship Program, Florida Endowment Fund. This program was created to encourage excellence in teaching and research through assistance to minority and female junior faculty. The program aims to help blacks and women who work in disciplines in which they are underrepresented. Recipients are provided a full year to pur-

sue special academic interest and/or research projects that will enhance their teaching and their tenure/promotion status at their home institutions. Twenty $15,000 fellowships are awarded annually to junior faculty. The awards are open to faculty in both public and private two-year and four-year colleges in the state. Since the program began in 1984, 72 fellowships have been awarded.
CONTACT: *Israel Tribble, Jr., President, (813) 864-4455.*

President's Fellowship Program, University of California. In order to improve the quality and diversity of the University of California faculty, to foster research, and to encourage outstanding minority men and women Ph.D. degree holders to pursue academic careers, in 1984 the Regents of the University of California established the President's Fellowship Program. The program offers postdoctoral fellowships to enhance the competitiveness of outstanding minority and women scholars for academic appointments at major research universities, such as the University of California, by assisting them to engage in research, and by providing mentoring and guidance toward advancement of their academic careers.
CONTACT: *Doris R. Fine, Principal Administrative Analyst, (415) 643-6507.*

The Carolina Minority Postdoctoral Scholars Program, the University of North Carolina at Chapel Hill. This program awards five or more postdoctoral research appointments for periods of up to two years on the Chapel Hill Campus. The awardees are expected to engage in essentially full-time research and teach not more than one course per year. Although the program encourages applications for study in any discipline represented on the campus, some preference is given to applicants in the humanities, social sciences, and fine arts where postdoctoral opportunities are seldom available.
CONTACT: *Dennis O'Connor, Vice Chancellor for Research and Dean of the Graduate School, (919) 962-1319.*

Chancellor's Minority Postdoctoral Fellowship Program, University of Illinois at Urbana–Champaign. This program is designed to increase underrepresented minority faculty on the Urbana campus. It provides postdoctoral fellowships, complemented by mentoring and guidance in preparing for an academic career, to underrepresented minority individuals.

Awards are made to applicants in all fields who show promise for tenure-track appointments on the Urbana-Champaign campus. Appointments are made for one academic year, with possible renewal for a second year.
CONTACT: *Joseph H. Smith, Associate Vice Chancellor for Academic Affairs, (217) 333-0805.*

Gaius Charles Bolin Fellowship, Williams College. The purpose of this award is to encourage minority Ph.D. candidates in the fields of humanities and natural, social, or behavioral sciences to pursue careers in college teaching. The award enables students to dedicate a considerable amount of their time to the completion of the dissertation. While the awardees are in residence at Williams College, they are expected to teach one one-semester course and are assigned a faculty advisor.
CONTACT: *John Reichert, Dean of Faculty, (413) 597-2351.*
(See also listings under *Professional Development* in Chapter 6, *Programs and Practices.*)

Resources

Handbook for Faculty Searches with Special Reference to Affirmative Action, The Ohio State University, 1987. A comprehensive 55-page manual on conducting faculty searches. Describes each phase of the search process, providing advice on effective techniques for conducting a fair and active search. **Copies are available from the Office of Academic Affairs or the Office of Human Relations, The Ohio State University, Columbus, OH.**

The University of California in the Twenty-First Century: Successful Approaches to Faculty Diversity, Joyce Justus, Project Director, 1987. This report and series of recommendations takes a "pipeline" approach, discussing strategies for success in an institutional effort to increase the representation of women and minorities in all aspects of the university. It includes an extensive section on faculty recruitment and retention, analyzing obstacles to progress and offering specific recommendations. **Copies are available for $4.50 from the President's Office University of California, Berkeley, CA 94720, (415) 642-6403.**

6

Administrators

Administrative officers occupy a unique position on campus, providing services to faculty, students, and the community. Given the wide range of administrative jobs on any campus, institutions will probably find it easier to recruit minority individuals for these positions than for faculty slots. Since the supply problem is not as great in the nonacademic areas, searches for persons to fill positions outside academic affairs should be easier. The business, administrative, development, and other parts of the institution have considerable flexibility to recruit individuals with different, but appropriate, credentials and work experience.

THE CURRENT SITUATION

While minority students comprised 16 percent of the students in higher education in 1985, only about 12 percent of all administrators were minority persons. It is important to note that this figure includes all the individuals who administered special minority programs in predominantly white institutions as well as all minority administrators in historically black institutions. If these groups were to be excluded from the 12 percent, the representation of minority administrators would be significantly lower.

Further, the representation of minority individuals has increased very slowly in recent years, as Table 4 indicates.

Another important dimension of the issue are the positions that minority administrators actually hold. The absence of minority individuals as presidents, vice presidents, and deans of predominantly white institutions is striking. Only two percent of predominantly white institutions are headed by blacks. Minority administrators generally hold "assistant to" or "minority" positions. They are often clustered in equal

Table 4: Percentages of higher education administrators by race/ethnicity: 1977, 1983, and 1985

	1977	1983	1985
Blacks	7.0	7.2	7.6
Hispanics	1.4	1.6	2.0
Asians	0.8	1.1	1.5
American Indians	0.3	0.3	0.4
All minority groups	9.5	10.2	11.5

Source: *Minorities in Higher Education: Fifth Annual Status Report* (Washington DC: American Council on Education: 1985), p. 35; and 1985 EEO-6 Detail Summary Report, p. 154.

opportunity programs, bilingual education, student services, and affirmative action, with little opportunity for career advancement. Too often, the special minority programs are funded with "soft money," leaving the administrators' jobs vulnerable.

STRATEGIES

Preliminary Steps

As with all other aspects of increasing minority participation on campus, increasing the number of minority administrators begins with the personal commitment of the president and/or governing board, certainly before an institution actually hire new administrators. Important preparatory steps include the following:

- *Begin by assessing the available pool, either nationally, regionally, or locally,* depending on the nature of institution. This information will help to establish some general goals of minority representation.

- *Examine recruitment and selection procedures.* Sometimes, the procedures in place are either an obstacle or simply not helpful in recruiting minority individuals. Are the current procedures yielding minority candidates? Are the minority candidates successful in getting to the interview stage? Not every position requires a search committee. Are attempts being made to identify talented individuals in the institution and to groom them for further responsibility?

- *Develop talent banks of minority professionals.* Many administrative positions are filled locally. Thus, identifying people in the local community with various expertise can provide a richer pool at the time of the search. The most effective talent banks are not simply lists of names. Personal contacts and first-hand information are very important in selecting the right individual for a particular assignment. Talent banks can also be national in scope, and names and background information can be collected through professional meetings and individual networks. The talent bank can be used not only to identify potential administrators, but also to identify consultants and speakers.

- *Train search committees and personnel recruiters.* People involved in the recruitment and selection process need to know how to translate this institutional priority into a reality. This involves discussions of the search process, how credentials are evaluated, and what particular requirements are stipulated for various administrative positions. Committees and recruiters can profit from discussions about how they will consider degrees from lesser known institutions, how they will apply formal education requirements for a particular position, and which evaluation criteria are useful in judging minority candidates. Affirmative action officers should be consulted on each search on how EEOC guidelines offer possibilities for assuring the fair and complete evaluation of minority candidates, and for assisting them in all phases of the search.

Role of the Hiring Official

Whether or not a search committee is used, the hiring official generally makes the final hiring decision. Certainly, an administrator who is attempting to fill an administrative vacancy can use all the techniques recommended below for enlarging the pool, screening candidates, and increasing the chances of finding and hiring minority candidates. In addition, when working with a search committee, the following steps in the process and approaches are important to consider:

- *The hiring official develops the job description.* While the job description may be modified by the committee in consultation with the hiring officials, he or she starts with this step. The educational and work experience requirements should flow from a clear job description.

■ *Presidents and hiring officials can exert pressure on committees to identify qualified minority candidates.* Many searches that have resulted in the hiring of minority candidates are the result of the strong personal commitment of the hiring official. Administrators who have specified to the search committee that a pool without minority representation or a short list without minority individuals will be unacceptable have usually gotten results. At one institution, the president insisted that *all* searches have a qualified minority or female candidate in the pool.

Role of the Search Committee

While not always necessary in the hiring process, most mid-level, and nearly all senior level appointments are made using search committees. The committee may play a variety of roles: screening only, searching and screening, or advising the hiring official about the recommended candidates. Whatever the role, the following practices are helpful:

■ *One individual—the chair or another person—has special responsibility for ensuring that the search identifies and seriously considers minority candidates.* That individual can serve as the "conscience" of the committee, whose responsibility to keep recruiting minority candidates high on the committee's agenda.

■ *One committee member is knowledgeable about federal and institutional guidelines for equal opportunity.* This person may be a representative of the affirmative action office, or a committee member who agrees to serve as an informed advocate. His or her role is to ensure that the committee's actions and deliberations conform to institutional policies and legal requirements.

■ *The committee clarifies essential qualifications and broadly defines the skills and experiences needed.* It is helpful to use generic skills (e.g., "excellent written and oral communication skills") rather than more specific, limiting ones (demonstrated ability to write promotional materials). The objective is not to make the qualifications vague, but rather to construct them in such a way that individuals who could succeed in the position are encourage to apply.

■ *It focuses on the tasks and responsibilities of the position in any advertisements.* Insisting on specific degrees, disciplines, and previous experience will narrow the pool.

■ *It weighs carefully the need for faculty rank and tenure as a qualification for an administrative position.* Clearly, most academic administrators do and should come from the faculty ranks. But it is not always essential. Positions within the academic domain, with responsibility for budgetary or personnel matters, do not necessarily require faculty experience. Also, positions in advancement, business, and student affairs are much less likely to require faculty experience for success.

■ *The committee considers the relative weights to be given to education, training, and experience.* It is useful for the committee members to discuss their preconceived notions of what qualifications the "most qualified" candidate should possess. What is the mixture of education, training, and experience in this "most qualified person." Why?

Enlarging the Pool

Searching for minority talent is the same as search for nonminority individuals. The key is to cast the net widely, use personal contacts, and tailor the effort to enlarge the pool to the particular administrative vacancy. An excellent reference on the search process is *The Search Committee Handbook,* described under *Programs and Practices* later in this chapter. Successful strategies to enlarge the pool include:

■ *Keeping track of prospective minority candidates, learning their career interests, and inviting them to apply for appropriate vacancies.* Personal networking and sponsorship typically work because they are based upon mutual trust and knowledge.

■ *Exhausting the possibilities for specialized advertising and direct mailings.* Resource guides and lists of minority professional groups are readily available. It is important to remember, however, that personal contacts are much more effective than such impersonal lists.

■ *Charging any consulting firm aiding in the search process to place high priority on the commitment to recruit minorities.* Consider retaining a firm that specializes in minority recruitment.

■ *Using a personal approach in contacting potential candidates.* The committee can begin by a brainstorming session for the names of possible resource persons, such as graduates, faculty, professional contacts, and community leaders. Knowledgeable individuals not on the committee should also be consulted. Each committee member can make a commitment to contact by telephone or in person a specific number of prospects each week, and report back to the committee.

- *Cultivating prospective candidates' interest in their institution.* Talented persons are often not looking actively for a new position. National and regional conferences, exchanges and consulting at institutions, and sustained contacts with recent minority graduates can help cultivate these prospects over the long term.

- *Using professional conference placement centers for preliminary interviews to expand the pool.* Attendance at minority professional conferences can often result in identifying candidates.

- *Looking outside higher education.* One of the primary reasons why there is more promise in increasing minority participation in administration is the fact that the search effort can move easily beyond conventional academic pipelines. Committees can find out where minority administrators are, seeking contacts with federal, state, and local government, and school districts. They can recruit minorities from the private sector. For example, experience in public relations may be highly beneficial in institutional advancement or communications. Experience in social work may be related to many roles in student services. Committees can also use job referral services or agencies that work outside of higher education.

- *Communicating with potential candidates.* Search committee members can informally convey encouragement and genuine interest in their candidacy. Much of the insight candidates need into the position is often provided informally.

- *Communicating with minority candidates throughout the process.*

Narrowing the Pool to the Short List

Once the candidate pool is developed, it is time to narrow the group to a much shorter list. The process will vary here. Some institutions develop a list of about 20 individuals, and ask for letters of reference at this point. Others will identify a lesser number to bring to the campus or interview by phone or off-site. This is the stage where committees need to think broadly and open-mindedly about the skills and competencies needed for the job.

Once the short list of candidates is developed, those candidates are invited to campus for interviews. It is tempting at this point to seek clear-cut criteria to lessen the ambiguity inherent in the process. However, it is important to once again think broadly about the skills and competencies needed for the job. Institutions that are effective in hiring minority administrators use most of the following strategies:

- *Address directly what qualifications the "most qualified" candidate will have.* Institutions determine what factors are most likely to predict success in the position. They also adhere to the original criteria established when the position was assessed and advertised.

- *Consider the potential evident in a minority person's record.* Committees can look beyond paper credentials and call for further information. They call references and gather sufficient information to make an informed decision before eliminating any minority from the pool.

- *They acknowledge and fight the inclination to avoid risk by selecting "known quantities."* They are careful when evaluating qualifications of individuals from lesser known institutions. Members of the search committee may have had no experience with predominantly black institutions or community colleges, both of which are likely sources of minority graduates and administrators.

- *Avoid conventional biases about what positions are "on the ladder" to the vacant position.* As a result of past hiring practices, many minority administrators have been pigeonholed into special program areas such as development education or minority student programs. Successful committees think broadly about the skills and competencies gained from a position. The admissions counselor who focused on minority recruitment may have cultivated the essential skills directly applicable to a position in the development office. Recognizing transferable skills is particularly important when evaluating candidacies from outside higher education.

The Interview Process

At this point, the search committee usually brings between five and ten individuals to campus. These numbers vary considerably, especially if off-site interviews were conducted. At the end of this process committees usually submit three names to the hiring official. It is important that these names be unranked, and that assessments of the candidates' strengths and weaknesses accompany the listing. Some points to remember:

- *Be sure at least one minority candidate makes it to the interview stage.* This is not to suggest that the interview be a token gesture. If a qualified minority candidate has not been identified as a finalist, the hiring official should strongly consider reopening the search.

- *Prepare for the interview by preparing a list of questions relevant to the position that will be asked of all candidates.* Examine the questions to determine whether any of them might have the effect of unfairly eliminating minority candidates. Search for any biases that may underlie questions or concerns about individual candidates.

- *Provide sufficient time for both the candidate and those involved in the hiring to gather the information necessary for informed decisions.* Arrange for both minority and majority candidates to meet with minority members of the community. This practice helps all candidates to understand the climate of the campus and surrounding community. It also provides an opportunity for minority administrators, staff, faculty, and students to form opinions about the candidate.

- *Ask candidates if they would like to meet with particular individuals or groups or if they have particular questions that might best be answered by individuals not included in the formal interview process.* Do not make assumptions about the candidate's interest in these contacts; rather, ask.

- *"Courting" is just as important for minority candidates as nonminority candidates.* Candidates react positively to being pursued as a potential employee, even when content with their current jobs. Each institution has its own methods of courting candidates for jobs, whether academic or administrative. Minorities who are identified as good prospects should be invited to campus receptions and functions, introduced to senior administrators, keep informed of campus developments, and routinely assured that the institution has a strong interest in hiring them.

Making an Offer

At this point, the decision is in the hands of the hiring official. If the decision is made to offer the position to a minority candidate, the following are considerations:

- *Market factors.* Institutions should be prepared to meet financially the market demand for minority administrators in a particular area. These considerations are analogous to the market considerations for faculty specialties in high demand.

- *Family visits.* When a national search has been conducted, and the position is being filled by an individual who is not in the local community, the candidate may wish to bring his or her family to the campus before making a final decision. Schools, religion, and housing are important factors for all individuals considering a move and a new job. This is true for majority as well as minority candidates. Generally, the need is especially great for minority candidates coming to a predominantly white community.

- *Spouse employment* Again, this may be a factor for any candidate. Institutions should specify what help, if any, they can provide.

- *Special institutional role for the minority administrator.* Often, minority administrators on predominantly white campuses have especially complex roles, and there are implicit, if not explicit, expectations of special relationships with the minority community and students beyond those stated in the job description. It is helpful to clarify and negotiate these prior to employment.

Retention and Advancement

Once an administrator is hired, he or she becomes part of the future talent pool. Retention of majority and minority administrators is generally the result of a good match, good conditions of employment (including especially a hospitable campus environment), and opportunity for growth and advancement. Successful strategies to retain minority administrators and help them advance include the following; as is the case for many strategies indicated in the *Handbook,* most represent good practices, applying to both majority and minority individuals:

- *Orientation of new minority administrative staff members.*
  Effective orientation helps employees understand the job,
  the administrative unit, the institution, and the community. If role expectations have been made explicit during
  the hiring process, there should be no surprises at this
  point. The institution should make both formal and
  informal efforts to welcome minority members to the
  community.

- *Aiming for a critical mass of minority staff.* Feeling of to-
  kenism and isolation among minorities can only be elimi-
  nated by more balanced ratios of minority and majority
  professionals on campus.

- *Identifying, grooming, and training talented minorities for
  senior roles.* Sponsorship is a well-established means of advancement for administrators, but it needs to be inten-
  tional in the case of minorities. The relationships will
  differ in intensity and duration, but may include role mod-
  eling, peer counseling, coaching, career advising, sponsoring, and serving as mentor. Sensitive attention to the
  quality of the relationships between majority supervisors
  and minority staff members is also required. Mutual ac-
  ceptance, comfortable interaction, and ease of communication cannot be assumed, but must be developed and
  nurtured.

- *Examining institutional policies and practices on internal
  promotion and advancement.* Most public institutions have
  written procedures guiding the filling of vacancies; all institutions have unwritten practices. These processes should
  be examined for unintended consequences that help or
  hinder the advancement of minority administrators. For
  example, newly created positions provide a readily available means to facilitate the advancement of minority persons.

- *Creating meaningful opportunities for professional growth
  and development, such as job rotations, institution-wide
  projects, and task forces.* Successful institutions consider
  opportunities carefully in terms of the developmental
  needs of the individual. Exposure to areas of central concern to the institution such as financial management, planning, and enrollment management are key developmental
  opportunities. They are especially important to enable mi-

norities to move out of narrowly defined roles such as minority counseling or special programs.

■ *Sponsoring minority administrators for national leadership development programs* such as the ACE Fellows program, Harvard's Institute for Educational Management, and Bryn Mawr's Summer Institute (described below). Institutional and regional opportunities for leadership training, internships, and networking among minority administrative staff are also very useful.

■ *Providing release time for administrators to pursue professional development.* Institutions might reduce the burden of committee service for a semester, or relieve the administrator from assigned duties to create time for special projects. Leaves to pursue graduate education are especially important for the advancement of minority administrators, who are less likely than majority administrators to have advanced degrees.

■ *Providing appropriate, timely, and constructive evaluation of performance.* Supervisors sometimes hesitate to offer constructive criticism to a minority staff member. Growth contracts or other formal mechanisms for evaluation can facilitate the evaluation process.

■ *Providing the needed financial support for travel, telephone, and professional memberships.* For minorities isolated in predominantly white campuses, maintaining professional associations may be particularly important for professional and personal support.

■ *Conducting exit interviews.* Learn why minority members chose to leave the institution, and use the information to initiate needed changes to enhance staff retention in the future.

CHECKLIST

For each of the strategies listed below, consider your response in light of the following questions:

■ If the answer is *yes,* is the strategy effective? How do you assess how well it is working? What outcome data are available?

- If the answer is *no,* would such an approach be useful on your campus? How high a priority would you place on developing such a policy or strategy?

Policy and Institutional Procedures

Suggested reviewers: governing board, president, senior officers, faculty senate, minority adminstrators.

1. Does the institution have an affirmative action officer or individual charged with the responsibilities of promoting equity? Does that individual have sufficient access to the president and senior officers? Does he or she have sufficient authority to be effective?

2. Is there an institution-wide policy affirming the institution's commitment to hiring minority individuals? Is this policy backed by any incentives or sanctions?

3. Is institutional progress in affirmative action regularly reviewed and discussed?

4. Is affirmative action incorporated in long-range planning efforts?

5. Are recruitment and selection procedures regularly reviewed to ensure that they foster the recruitment of minority candidates?

6. Are search committees and consultants trained to assist them in their efforts to recruit minority personnel?

Enlarging the Pool

Suggested reviewers: search committee members, hiring officials, affirmative action officers. (These individuals are the suggested reviewers for all subsequent parts of the checklist.)

1. Do administrators develop a network of prospective minority candidates and referral sources on an ongoing basis that they can tap when positions open?

2. Does the job description focus on the tasks and responsibilities of the position rather than on past experience and paper qualifications?

3. Are special efforts made to expand the notification of job vacancies to ensure that minority candidates apply?

4. Do members of the search committee or the hiring official identify prospective minority candidates through a variety of networks?

5. Are potential minority candidates contacted personally?

Screening the Candidate Pool

1. Does the committee or hiring official specify the most important qualifications as a basis for screening dossiers?

2. Are potential sources of bias openly aired in the committee, for example, the importance of degrees from prestigious institutions?

3. Are steps taken to ensure that criteria are uniformly applied to all candidates?

4. Has the hiring official required that a minority be included on the short list?

The Interview Process

1. Are all candidates asked the same questions? Are they all relevant to the position?

2. Do minority candidates have the opportunity to meet with other minority persons on campus? to receive information about the minority community?

Making an Offer

1. Is the salary competitive given market demands for minority candidates in particular positions?

2. Is spouse employment an issue? Is the institution prepared to help?

3. Are there special expectations (implicit or explicit) of the minority administrator because he or she is minority? Have these expectations been openly discussed?

Retention and Advancement

1. Do minority administrators received adequate orientation to the position, the institution, and the community?

2. Are talented minority administrators identified and groomed for future leadership roles? How?

3. Are institutional policies on internal promotion and advancement regularly reviewed to determine their effect on minority administrators?

4. Are there meaningful opportunities for minority administrators to experience professional growth on the job?

5. Are professional development opportunities available for minority administrators? sufficiently funded?

6. When minority administrators leave the institution, are efforts made to determine the reason?

PROGRAMS AND PRACTICES

Recruiting

Affirmative Action Recruitment Awards Program, State University of New York. This program was designed and funded by the New York State/United Professions Affirmative Action Committee, comprised of representatives from United University Professions, the State University of New York (SUNY) Central Administration, and the Governor's Office of Employee Relations. It is intended to assist campus recruitment efforts to attract more minorities, women, disabled people, and Vietnam-era veterans to SUNY academic and professional employee positions in the bargaining unit. The program provides a travel stipend of up to $1,000 to eligible academic and professional employees to attend events specifically for the purpose of recruiting employees from these underrepresented groups.
CONTACT: *Steven Moskowitz, Staff Director, New York State/United University Professions Joint Labor-Management Committees, (518) 457-1198.*

Professional Development

Campus programs
Affirmative Action Leave Program, State University of New York. Begun in 1987–88, this program provides leaves prior to tenure or permanent appointment review, thus permitting recipients time away from campus to complete projects or study programs likely to improve their chances of attaining tenure or permanent or continuing appointment. Leaves for one semester or longer, as required, may be granted with the permission and support of the recipient's campus. Persons targeted for assistance are members of minority groups, women, disabled people and Vietnam-era veterans. Members of these groups are in short supply at many SUNY campuses, and many give generously of their time to service activities at the expense of completing their own degrees, certifications, research and publications. This program is designed to help them compensate for the disadvantage in the tenure review or permanent appointment process that may result from their service commitments.
CONTACT: *Joyce Yaple Villa, Assistant Vice Chancellor for Employee Relations, (518) 443-5684.*

The Administrative Fellows Program, California State University (CSU) System. The Administrative Fellows Program was developed in 1978 to provide administrative training to ethnic, minority and women faculty and staff through mentor relationships and training workshops. Up to 12 full-time CSU faculty and staff members are selected by a system-wide committee from applicants nominated by the campus presidents. The administrative fellows are matched with CSU senior administrators who agree to serve as their mentors for an academic year. The mentors provide guidance as well as opportunities for the fellows to be actively involved in administration of campus programs. Throughout the year, the fellows attend workshops that provide additional training on various aspects of higher education administration. Of the 120 participants, 74 (62 percent), have advanced in their careers. **CONTACT:** *Dr. Tim T. L. Dong, State University Dean, (213) 590-5603.*

National programs

Administrative Fellows Program, the Woodrow Wilson National Fellowship Foundation. Established in 1967, the Administrative Fellows Program is designed to increase the pool of qualified professionals to address academic and financial concerns in colleges serving disadvantaged groups. Colleges eligible to participate are those schools that have been designated as "developing institutions" for the purposes of receiving Title III funds from the Department of Education. The fellows are full-time administrators who serve in positions such as assistant to the president, business manager, or director of research, planning, and development. Once selected as a finalist, the fellow's skills, expertise, and interests are matched with position descriptions received from participating institutions. Fellows' assignments focus on the crucial problem of balancing cost and income while maintaining operational efficiency and educational effectiveness. Fellows are afforded the opportunity both to contribute directly to the institution, and to work in an environment in which their management skills may be honed and professional development accelerated. The Woodrow Wilson National Fellowship Foundation provides a salary subsidy to the participating institutions to supplement the negotiated salary of the Fellow. **CONTACT:** *Dr. Sulayman Clark, Vice President for Minority Programs, (609) 924-4666.*

American Council on Education Fellows Program. The Fellows Program identifies and prepares promising leaders in higher education. Approximately 30 fellows are selected each year through a national competition. Candidates are typically faculty or administrators such as department chair, or assistant or associate dean; they must be nominated by the president of their institutions. Fellows spend a year as a intern with a college president and senior officers, who are formally designated as mentors. The fellow's salary is paid by the sponsoring institution; the host college or university pays the travel and seminar expenses. Preferably, fellows intern on a different campus from their own but they may remain on their home campus if released from all previous responsibilities. Fellows attend three week-long seminars on management and leadership issues, develop their own regional meetings, and travel extensively to other campuses. Since its inception in 1965, nearly 900 individuals have participated. Nominations of minority candidates are actively sought. During the last five years, women half comprised nearly half the fellows, and minorities more than 20 percent. Deadline for nominations and applications is November 15 each year. **CONTACT:** *Donna McDoniel or Irene Itabashi, ACE Fellows Program, (202) 939-9420.*

Institute for Educational Management (IEM), Harvard University. This four-week program is conducted on the Harvard campus each July. The case study courses, in areas such as marketing, financial management, planning, labor relations, and higher education law, are designed to provide participants with a broad view of higher education administration with a focus on the unique policy-setting responsibilities of senior executives. Most participants are presidents, vice presidents, or deans in both academic and nonacademic fields. During the past five years, women have averaged 30 percent of each class, while minorities have averaged 24 percent. **CONTACT:** *Sharon McDade, Director, (617) 495-2655.*

Management Development Program (MDP), Harvard University. In 1986, IEM launched the Management Development Program, a two-week institute for middle-level academic and nonacademic administrators. It is designed to broaden management participants' perspectives and leadership skills while they explore the mission of higher education in today's society. Participants typically are in middle-level to first-tier senior positions, with the majority holding titles such as department chair, director, assistant and associate dean, dean, as-

sistant and associate vice presidents. The classes of 85 participants have averaged 44 percent women and 27 percent minorities.
CONTACT: *Sharon McDade, Director, (617) 495-2655.*

College Management Program (CMP), Carnegie-Mellon University. Launched in 1976, this three-week institute for academic and nonacademic administrators addresses issues such as strategic planning, management, marketing, budgeting, financial analysis, situational leadership, decisionmaking, and the personal computer as a management tool. The CMP capitalizes on the management and computer science strengths of Carnegie-Mellon University.
CONTACT: *Henry Faulk, Director, Associate Dean for Executive Education, CMU, (412) 268-2198.*

Higher Education Resource Services (HERS)/Bryn Mawr and Wellesley. HERS supports two national institutes specifically for women in both academic and nonacademic jobs. Since 1976, the Summer Institute for Women in Higher Education Administration, co-sponsored by HERS/Mid-America and Bryn Mawr College, has groomed women faculty and middle managers for senior management positions. This four-week program is held at Bryn Mawr College. A program similar in content is offered by HERS/New England at Wellesley College. Participants attend a series of five seminars over a period of a year. Both programs devote significant attention to career development for participants, as well as dealing with management and leadership in higher education.
CONTACT: *Cynthia Secor or Margeret Healy, Co-Directors, HERS Summer Institute for Women, Bryn Mawr, (215) 645-6161* or *Cynthia Secor, Director, HERS/New England, (617) 235-0320, ext. 2829.*

Kellogg National Fellowship Program, W. K. Kellogg Foundation. This annual program offers outstanding professionals an opportunity to broaden their social and intellectual sensitivity, awareness, and leadership potential. The three-year program is designed for individuals who are in the early years of their professional careers. Fellows are drawn from business, education, human service agencies, and private practice. They spend approximately 25 percent of their time on fellowship-related activities, including a self-designed learning plan for personal and professional development. Fellows also participate in group seminars sponsored by the

Foundation. The fellow's employer is reimbursed 12.5 percent of the fellow's annual salary (not to exceed an aggregate
of $20,000 for the three-year period).
CONTACT: *Kellogg National Fellowship Program, W. K.
Kellogg Foundation, (616) 968-1611.*

Resources

Administrative searches
**Theodore J. Marchese, assisted by Jane F. Lawrence. *The
Search Committee Handbook: A Guide to Recruiting Administrators.* Washington DC: American Association for Higher
Education, 1987, 57 pp.** A comprehensive manual on the
search process. Chapters cover the vacancy, the committee,
the job, the search, the screening, the interviews, the appointment. Copies are available from the American Association
for Higher Education, One Dupont Circle, Suite 600, Washington, DC 20036, (202) 293-6440, $8.95 per copy; discounts
available for bulk orders.

Professional development
**Sharon A. McDade, *Higher Education Leadership, Enhancing
Skills through Professional Development Programs.* ASHE-
ERIC Higher Education Report No. 5, Washington DC: Association for the Study of Higher Education, 1987, 121 pp.**
Contains an analysis of professional development issues, in-
cluding discussion of career paths and administrative skills,
as well as a description of the leading national professional
development programs. Copies can be obtained from the
publications Department, ASHE-ERIC Higher Education
Reports, the George Washington University, One Dupont
Circle, Suite 630, Washington, DC 20036, (202) 296-2597,
$10.00 prepaid and $7.50 for AERA, AAHE, AIR, and
ASHE members.

7

Campus Climate

Campus climate embraces the culture, habits, decisions, practices, and policies that make up campus life. It is the sum total of the daily environment, and central to the "comfort factor" that minority students, faculty, staff, and administrators experience on campus. Students and other members of the campus community who feel unwelcome or alienated from the mainstream of campus life are unlikely to remain. If they do remain, they are unlikely to be successful.

The culture or climate of an organization cannot be quantified or legislated. It is shaped by tradition, values, and attitudes, many of which are unexpressed. Thus, changing the campus climate can be a difficult and elusive task. But, because the climate is so central to all other efforts to improve minority participation, it is both the point of departure and the culmination of all other efforts.

THE CURRENT SITUATION

The past few years have brought a disturbing increase of racially and ethnically motivated violence and conflict on campuses across the country. Widely covered in the national press, these incidents were disheartening evidence that our nation's campuses can be not only unconcerned or unfriendly to minority students, but even downright hostile.

An inhospitable campus environment can be overt and conspicuous, or quite subtle. Some campuses have experienced outright verbal and physical conflict motivated by racial or ethnic issues. These incidents must be dealt with decisively through campus disciplinary and legal procedures. Failure to do so constitutes a clear message that intolerance can flourish and that the ethos of the campus is not sufficiently powerful to prevent individuals from acting on their prejudices.

113

More frequently, the problems are subtle. Minority students often feel marginal, conspicuous, and isolated from the mainstream of the institution. The scarcity of minority students, faculty and administrators is perceived as institutional indifference to minority issues. The absence of minority focus in the curriculum is interpreted as a devaluation of diversity. These environmental problems may compound any academic difficulties experienced by minority students. Thus, minority students often find it doubly difficult to feel comfortable in the campus majority culture.

At the same time, majority students are often unaware of the experiences of minorities on campus. In a recent survey of one urban campus, 76 percent of the black students, but only 36 percent of the white students, thought that discrimination against blacks was still a problem on campus. The study also revealed that 71 percent of the black students thought the white graduates of that institution had a better chance of getting the job of their choice, while 34 percent of the white students held this opinion. This difference in perception is significant. White students, faculty, and administrators often do not see the environment in the same way as minority individuals.

Another contributor to tensions in the campus climate is the reaction of majority students to minority student behaviors. When minority students gather by themselves in the cafeteria or student union, white students may perceive them as separatist or hostile. Similar assumptions are not made about majority students gathering by themselves.

The evidence of an inhospitable campus environment may be clear or a matter of nuance. Thus, it is important to train all members of the campus community to be sensitive to climate issues and to face them squarely, rather than ignore them.

STRATEGIES

Improving the campus climate is everyone's responsibility. The climate sets the tone and the pace for efforts to recruit and retain minority students, faculty, and administrators. Because everyone on campus is a participant in the effort, the strategies outlined below are directed toward specific campus groups. However, underlying the particular strategies are some general principles that apply to all.

General Strategies for Success

- *Recognize climate as an issue.* No campus is free of racial or ethnic prejudice. On occasion, it takes a virulent and destructive turn through name calling, derogatory stories in the campus press, graffiti, or violence. Often, signs of an inhospitable environment are more subtle. They may seem trivial—jokes or personal discomfort exhibited by whites with minorities—but they are important and should be seriously considered as elements of the campus climate.

- *Recognize that the issue belongs to everyone on campus.* Changing the campus climate requires leadership from the president and board as well as commitment and leadership throughout the campus. The active involvement of senior faculty is particularly important in effecting any campus change.

- *Provide education and training.* Making people aware of the issue is a crucial first step. Training programs for administrators, faculty, staff, security personnel, and students can help sensitize people of all races to the perceptions and feelings of others. Climate issues are as much about perception as they are about "reality." Workshops, symposia, films, and student activities are possible mechanisms.

- *Involve students.* Students are the most important players in improving campus climate. Student leaders can initiate activities such as workshops, residential programs, or lecture series, and put this high on the agenda for the entire campus community.

- *Keep an eye on the classroom.* The central experience for all students is in the classroom. Thus, faculty are key. Overt faculty prejudice can result in inappropriate racial or ethnic remarks in class or in lowering the performance of alienated or discouraged minority students. Also, professors' unconscious assumptions that minority students are unable to perform up to par may become self-fulfilling prophecies. Or, more subtle behaviors such as different treatment of minority students, dissimilar eye contact, and other non-verbal behaviors may be equally negative for minority students. For example, do white professors call on minority students for class participation as frequently as they call on majority students? Do they ask them the same kinds of questions? Do they pay the same attention to minority students when they do speak? Do they provide equally specific feedback on assignments? Do professors value students' papers addressing ethnic or racial issues as much as others? It is important to deal with the issue of classroom climate as well as to recognize it; it can be introduced at faculty meetings, workshops, or other faculty activities to ensure that it is put on everyone's agenda. (See Chapter 8 for further discussion of this topic.)

■ *Actions speak louder than words.* Creating a hospitable campus environment requires going beyond the announcement of good intentions and uplifting principles. Hiring practices, reward systems, and the inclusion of minorities in all phases of campus life are the proof of the pudding. For example, a racially and ethnically mixed senior administrative staff is a visible sign from the president that he or she has a personal and institutional stake in improving minority participation.

■ *Pay attention to symbols.* Campus traditions or rituals are important symbols. For example, a confederate flag may symbolize southern regional pride to some, but, for many, it is an overt reminder of slavery and prejudice. A fraternity "slave auction" may be perceived as a harmless parody by some, but be deeply offensive to many.

■ *Build a critical mass of minorities on campus.* Research has shown that "multicultural campuses" (campuses with 30 percent or more minority enrollment) are most conducive to the success of minority students. While 30 percent is not a realistic goal on most campuses, the fact remains that if there is only a handful of minority students, faculty, and administrators, they are much more likely to feel isolated. Extra efforts will be needed to make minority students feel welcome on those campuses where there are only a few minority individuals.

■ *Cultivate pluralism in cultural and extracurricular activities.* Minority speakers, performers, and participants in campus activities will enrich the event and constitute an important minority presence on campus. It is also important that minority speakers and visitors be associated with a wide variety of issues and topics, and not only with minority issues.

■ *Establish a policy concerning bias and bias incidents.* The policy should explicitly prohibit harassment, discrimination, and other manifestations of bias, specify disciplinary mechanisms, and be communicated to the entire campus.

- **Develop a mechanism for reporting prejudice-motivated incidents.** The information gathered through the reporting process will help discern patterns and track trends. While confidentiality may be an issue, it is generally helpful for this information to be available to the campus community for educational purposes. The State Of New York Governor's Task Force on Bias-Related Violence (1988) recommended "that institutions should experiment with modes of widely reporting the outcomes of disciplinary processes in cases of strong campus interest and concern (p. 63)."

- **Establish a sound grievance procedure.** A grievance procedure for students, faculty, and administrators should include a statement of policy, a definition of what constitutes a breach of that policy, and explicit sanctions for offenses. An ombudsperson or advocate to help individuals navigate the formal grievance process, as well as to resolve problems informally, is also very helpful. Be sure that the campus community knows about the ombudsperson and the procedures in place through printed materials, workshops, or other means.

- **Establish a mechanism for dispute resolution.** It is likely that disputes will arise on a pluralistic campus. Establishing a mechanism to resolve disputes and to prevent the escalation of disputes is very useful, and may be key to achieving harmony in a pluralistic environment.

Strategies for Presidents

- **Begin with a strong leadership initiative.** Presidents play an active an visible role in improving the campus climate. Board support is essential. Presidents might begin with a major campus address and the announcement of the board policy on improving minority participation and the campus climate. The policy should state explicitly that racist acts toward minority individuals will not be tolerated by the institution and will be subject to quick and firm disciplinary action. Beyond the statement of good intentions, leaders can take the initiative to mobilize the campus community, to put into place programs and activities that can accomplish the stated goals.

- **Promote racial diversity among leadership.** As indicated above, the old saying that actions speak louder than words is especially true with respect to campus climate. The president who actively recruits minority individuals for major administrative positions is sending a powerful message about personal and institutional commitment.

- *Designate an individual responsible for institution-wide efforts to ensure an equitable and hospitable climate for minority persons.* Be sure that the person has access to top administrators as well as some decision-making authority, and is known to the entire campus community.

- *Ensure that all faculty and staff are aware of services available to minority persons on campus, and know when and how to make appropriate referrals.* Often, services and programs exist that are not well known throughout the campus, such as complaint mechanisms, financial aid counseling, remedial programs, or support services. Also, the campus community should be made aware of special services and activities available especially to minority students, such as an ethnic cultural center, peer support groups, and minority mentors.

- *Be sure that there is continual evaluation of efforts and monitoring of campus climate.* Evaluation mechanisms may include surveys of students, faculty, and staff concerning changes in campus climate; interviews and surveys of students who drop out or transfer; monitoring trends in racially and ethnically motivated incidents.

Strategies for Administrators and Faculty

- *Develop educational materials and programs.* These efforts, which might include printed materials, workshops, or films, should identify behaviors that contribute to an inhospitable environment. They can illustrate the adjustment problems many minorities face on campus, and generally develop a new sensitivity to climate issues among majority students, faculty, and administrators. Faculty development programs and training of teaching assistants might also include information on differential treatment of minority students in the classroom. Groups who would benefit from such training are advisors, career counselors, administrative staff, and security personnel. These programs should be made available to all members of the campus community. They can be incorporated into regular in-service training courses for staff or the ongoing freshman orientation for students, and thus not be seen as "special" or "separate," but part of the ongoing educational process.

■ *Provide adequate financial and human resources to improve the campus climate.* Institutions seeking to improve campus climate can expect to incur expenses to develop materials, bring individuals on campus, and devote adequate personnel to the job.

■ *Form information-sharing networks with other institutions that are trying to improve climate.* Borrow and adapt the successes of others; analyze what works, what doesn't, and why.

■ *Interview students who transfer, drop out, or change majors.* Was climate an issue? Could the student's departure have been prevented? How?

■ *Integrate academic concerns with student life.* Faculty may be tempted to view campus climate as the province of student affairs personnel. Integration of the two through frequent communication will strengthen efforts to improve campus climate.

■ *Develop criteria about climate issues to be used in evaluating applicants for faculty and staff positions.* This is particularly important for senior administrators. Examples of such criteria are specific accomplishments in addressing the issue of campus climate in the individual's previous position or proposals to do so in the new position.

■ *Include climate issues in performance evaluations of faculty and staff.* This is particularly relevant for staff who are in direct contact with students, such as faculty, security personnel, cafeteria personnel, receptionists, and counselors.

■ *Recognize individuals and organizational units for exceptional progress in creating a positive climate for minority persons, just as other forms of outstanding performance are recognized.*

Strategies for Student Affairs Administrators

Student affairs personnel have a special role to play in improving campus climate. While the task should never be theirs alone, it is also true that the nature of their work and their personal contact with students made them particularly valuable contributors to the effort. In particular, student affairs personnel can:

- *Review extracurricular programs and organizations to ensure that they meet the needs of minority students.* Sororities and fraternities, student clubs and programs can foster minority participation on campus. Their effect may also be negative if they are discriminatory, offensive, or unfriendly to minority persons. Student affairs personnel can work with fraternity and sorority advisors to establish and implement guidelines to ensure that their standards of behavior and membership practices are neither discriminatory nor offensive.

- *Survey the residential climate for minority persons in all institution-owned housing.* Identify specific problems and design programs or policies to correct them.

- *Make sure that resident hall advisors are sensitive to climate issues and receive training.*

- *Hold workshops on climate for all students in residence halls.*

- *Encourage the development and activities of minority organizations on campus.* These might include social organizations, academic and cultural groups, or other organizations that provide peer support for minority individuals or foster an appreciation of minority culture. Majority students, faculty, and staff should be encouraged to attend events featuring minority speakers or issues.

- *Encourage minority students to participate and seek leadership positions in extracurricular activities.*

- *Provide minority students with opportunities to acquire the skills necessary to seek leadership positions.* Appointing students to task forces and committees creates an important growth opportunity for all students; these experiences are especially important for minority students.

- *Monitor student government spending to ensure that minority organizations and programs are funded at appropriate levels.*

- *Encourage cooperative programming between minority and majority student organizations (such as Greek-letter organizations).*

Strategies for Faculty

Faculty are responsible for the climate in their classrooms. Campus climate is closely tied to the teaching and learning process; the larger institutional climate cannot be separated from what happens in individual classrooms. Strategies to help faculty make their classrooms and teaching as helpful as possible to minority students are developed in Chapter 8. Other useful approaches that apply to faculty members are described in other sections of this chapter.

Strategies for Students

- *Develop formal and informal groups of minority students for academic and social support.*

- *Sponsor cultural events featuring minority individuals and issues.* These events can be part of an ongoing lecture or event series, or separately sponsored by minority student groups. In either case, it is important to encourage majority students to attend these events.

- *Implement peer counseling programs.*

- *Plan a special orientation for new minority students.*

- *Include minority students in the campus-wide student orientation program.* Have a portion of the orientation address sensitivity to racial, ethnic, and cultural differences.

- *Communicate minority student concerns freely and openly to administrators and faculty.*

CHECKLIST

The following questions can be applied to each of the items below to determine its value and applicability for your campus:

- If the answer is *yes,* is the strategy or policy effective? What is the process you use to assess how well it is working? What outcome data do you have?
- If the answer is *no,* would such an approach be important or useful to your institution to improve minority participation? How high a priority would you place on developing such a policy or strategy?

Board Composition and Campus-wide Policies

Suggested reviewers: the governing board and president.

1. Does the membership of the governing board include minority individuals?

2. Has the governing board developed a policy supporting the vigorous recruitment of minorities on campus, explicitly prohibiting racist acts, and specifying disciplinary procedures and sanctions?

3. Is there a campus committee charge with analyzing and making recommendations to improve campus climate?

4. Are there methods in place to assess campus climate regularly and to report the findings to the campus community?

5. Is there a mechanism in place to resolve disputes?

Institutional Structures and Procedures

Suggested reviewers: president, administrators, faculty, students.

1. Is there a particular individual responsible for monitoring issues of campus climate? Does that person have access to top-level administrators?

2. Is there an ombudsperson to mediate situations of racial and ethnic tensions before they become serious problems or enter into the grievance system?

3. Are there vehicles for communications among academic departments, student services, and minority students and organizations to discuss climate on campus?

4. Are funds available to departments and units that wish to sponsor events of interest to the minority community on campus?

5. Are there ways to determine if minority students feel uncomfortable or excluded in the classroom or on campus?

6. Are institutional publications reviewed for overt and subtle racism?

Mediation and Grievance Procedures

Suggested reviewers: Same as above.

1. Is there a grievance procedure for issues of racial or ethnic discrimination or bias? Is it the same one used for other grievances? Why, or why not?

2. Are the grievance procedure and its results reviewed periodically to determine the speed of resolution and whether or not the parties considered the process to be fair?

3. Are there routine mechanisms to anticipate "minor" con-

cerns (e.g., negative faculty attitudes, problematic dormitory relationships) before they escalate to the formal grievance stage?

Student Life

Suggested reviewers: student affairs personnel, faculty, students.

1. Do minority students regularly participate in extracurricular activities such as clubs, service groups, newspapers, and so forth? Are efforts made to increase minority participation?

2. Are efforts made to ensure that student entertainment and activity programs reflect the interests of minority students and feature minority artists and speakers?

3. If there is a local minority community, is it involved in the cultural life of the campus?

4. Are campus organizations and fraternities and sororities monitored to determine if they are congenial to minority students and whether minority students are encouraged to participate? How is this accomplished?

5. Is there minority student participation on institutional committees and task forces that have student representation?

6. Are common student funds made available to minority student organizations on an equitable basis with other student organizations?

Education and Training

Suggested reviewers: student affairs personnel in particular, as well as all other members of the campus community.

1. Are there training materials on campus climate? Are they incorporated into the regular training of administrators and staff? into faculty development programs? student orientation? Are they widely and regularly used?

2. Is information routinely supplied to all faculty on services available to minority individuals on campus, and on the appropriate referral process for using them?

3. Is training on campus climate issues provided to the following groups: Students? Faculty? Deans and department chairs? Residence hall and dining hall personnel? Campus security personnel? Advisors? Counselors?

PROGRAMS AND PRACTICES

Task Force on Human Relations, University of Alabama at Tuscaloosa. In an effort to develop a focal point for awareness of race relations at the University of Alabama, in 1986 President Joab L. Thomas established a Task Force on Race Relations. The Task Force includes chairpersons of several standing committees of the university and of student government as well as three members of the local community. Its primary duties include reviewing activities and initiatives on campus and disseminating information to appropriate standing committees and designated units in their efforts to improve race relations. It also helps to coordinate activities across the campus. Although the group changed its name to Task Force on Human Relations to expand its involvement beyond areas of race relations, it still maintains racial and ethnic issues as a central concern. A report on the first six months has been issued.
CONTACT: *Dean William H. Macmillan, the Graduate School, (205) 348-5921.*

The Madison Plan, University of Wisconsin–Madison. The Madison Plan is a comprehensive plan to increase minority participation in all aspects of the university. A significant component of the plan, Non-Discriminatory Environment, contains several initiatives, including: (1) broadening existing student disciplinary policy so that special or more severe sanctions may be sought when a violation of existing student conduct rules involves the race, religion, color, creed, gender, disability, sexual orientation, national origin, or ancestry of the victim; (2) the creation of a nondisciplinary mediation and counseling program which will respond to cases where racial harassment is alleged but disputed or unproved; (3) the adoption of a policy on harassment by the University's Faculty Senate and academic Staff Assembly to govern the conduct of the faculty and academic staff. These and other initiatives are aimed at providing a climate that is not intimidating, hostile or demeaning to anyone.

CONTACT: *Bernard C. Cohen, Vice Chancellor for Academic Affairs, or Mary K. Rouse, Dean of Students, (608) 262-1234.*

University of Maryland, Baltimore County (UMBC) Campus. A series of activities has been initiated on the UMBC campus in the last several years to improve minority participa-

tion. In 1986, a survey was conducted by the National Institute Against Prejudice and Violence to determine the campus community's perceptions of the climate. The results were widely disseminated. During the following year, the campus held three open forums on racial, religious, and ethnic tolerance. A seminar "From Understanding to Action: Strategies for Reducing Intergroup Tension" included such topics as strategies for preventing and reducing conflict; responding to incidents of harassment and violence; and stereotyping. Training sessions were also offered for residential life personnel, and the student handbook was revised to reflect the campus' commitment to pluralism. In 1988, Chancellor Michael Hooker created the Chancellor's Advisory Committee on Human Relations which reviews, monitors, and makes recommendations regarding desegregation and affirmative action efforts. The committee is also charged with developing deeper appreciation of, and respect for, the diversity of the UMBC community. Periodically, the Office of the Chancellor provides the UMBC community with a progress report.
CONTACT: *Susan T. Kitchen, Vice Chancellor for Student Affairs, (301) 455-2393.*

University of Michigan–Ann Arbor. The University of Michigan (UM) has undertaken a number of initiatives to promote a culture that nourishes racial, ethnic, and cultural diversity. Significant actions by the university include establishing an Office of Minority Affairs which has developed programs addressing access, process, achievement, and transfer; adopting an antiracial harassment policy and a grievance mechanism to collect data on racial incidents; addressing cultural and racial diversity in student orientation programs; and developing an educational program for UM staff members aimed at valuing and preserving diversity. Films, lectures, human relations workshops, visiting scholars, exhibits and other programs designed to increase multicultural communication and an understanding of minority concerns among all students are presented in residence halls as well as throughout the campus community. In addition to these programs, UM teaching assistants participate in workshops that are designed to teach them how to recognize and combat racial and other forms of prejudice in the classroom. All of these efforts to change the culture are part of a planned change strategy.
CONTACT: *Office of Minority Affairs, (313) 936-1055.*

The Northeast Consortium of Colleges & Universities (NECCUM). In 1988, NECCUM established an institute designed to provide professionals in such fields as education, medicine, and social work with an exploration of the language and culture of the Hispanic Caribbean. Participants are professionals who serve a growing number of Hispanic immigrants to Massachusetts, particularly from the Dominican Republic. This program is designed to help them understand and appreciate Hispanic culture. The institute focuses on language immersion and the humanistic study of history, politics, the arts, culture, and lifestyle of that part of the world. Special attention is given to social and cultural issues such as the Immigration Experience, Contributions of Hispanic Cultural Heritage to New England Society, and Intercultural Interaction. The institute involves three phases. Phase 1 includes five seminars providing a background in history, politics, culture and language of the Caribbean. Phase 2 comprises three weeks' study in the Dominican Republic concentrating on language, customs, literature and local society. In Phase 3, the local community serves as the audience for the oral, written, dramatic, and artistic presentations by the participants in the first two phases of the institute. In this way, the educational institutions, businesses, and the Hispanic communities work together: (1) to study the Hispanic cultural experience as it is expressed in the Caribbean and as it contributes to the multicultural society; and (2) to relate that learning to the diverse communities in Massachusetts, thereby improving intercultural dialogue. The pilot program was conducted in 1988; plans to repeat it are not yet established.
CONTACT: *Patricia Karl, (617) 686-3183.*

Committee to Advance Our Common Purposes, Rutgers University. In October 1987, the committee was established to improve cohesion in the university community, in part through reducing prejudice and bigotry, particularly racism, sexism, and homophobia on campus. Rutgers University President Edward J. Bloustein charged the committee with the following responsibilities: assessment of patterns of prejudice on campus; administration of a grant program (described below); supervision of several program efforts underway or anticipated; and coordination of an agenda for action previously proposed by the president. The full committee met three times; several meetings of the executive

committee and other subgroups were also held to consider or initiate action in the following areas: assessment, grant program, curriculum, staff and faculty development, student relations, and commemorative events.
CONTACT: *Donald R. Peterson, Chair, (201) 932-2186/2016.*

Promoting our Common Purpose Grant Program, Rutgers University. As on of the committee activities described above, the Rutgers University grant program initiated in 1988 solicits proposals from "students and student organizations to develop programs to eliminate bigotry and prejudice and to foster appreciation for the diversity of our community." Award of more than $41,000 were made to 24 projects on the three Rutgers campuses. Among the awardees were the Rutgers Association of Philippine Students and eight other student associations for production of *Asian Faces,* a literary magazine; a Latin American film scholars program, sponsored by the Hispanic Affairs and Latin American Program, Latin American Students Organization, and the Social Work Department; and a lecture series "Racism in an Anthropological Perspective," sponsored by the Anthropology Club.
CONTACT: *Kimberly Wicks, Queens Campus, (201) 932-7255.*

Resources

Education Program to Increase Racial Awareness (EPIRA), University of California–Santa Barbara (UCSB). EPIRA is a training program designed to help facilitate racial awareness among faculty, staff, and students. The program incorporates the use of a videotape and a discussion facilitator. The videotape is used to stimulate discussion about the experience of minority students on the UCSB campus. After the videotape is presented, the facilitator guides group discussion by raising some of the issues highlighted in the tape. The program establishes the project goals and provides written suggestions to facilitators on how to manage large groups.
CONTACT: *Harleen W. McAda, Assistant Vice Chancellor, Student Affairs Special Programs, (805) 961-2771.*

Black By Popular Demand is a half-hour videotape that discusses issues involving the academic, financial, and social aspects of black student life on a predominantly white campus. Produced on the Iowa State University campus, the program presents commentary from students, faculty, staff, and administration to evoke thought and ultimately action in resolving situations that exist for the black student community. Created entirely by black students as their voice to the university, the program's goal is to initiate an awareness of issues black students and the university community must face. The videotape is also designed to motivate black students by generating an understanding of their role and position within the university setting. The film can be used as a catalyst for group discussions within a meeting format and raises issues on institutional racism, academic support and preparation, student apathy, and the undermining of financial support structures. The film can be purchased or rented. **CONTACT:** *David Kooker, Redshoes Productions, P.O. Box 1223, Welch Avenue Station, Ames, IA 50010, (515) 292-1883.*

Gayle Pemberton. *On Teaching the Minority Student: Problems and Strategies.* **Bowdoin College, 1988.** This 27-page essay, written by a black professor, discusses the issues related to teaching minority students on predominantly white campuses. Directed to faculty members, it raises issues of classroom climate, teacher expectations, and student behaviors. Pemberton recommends strategies to guide faculty in helping students achieve their maximum potential. *Copies are available from Bowdoin College, Brunswick, ME 04011.*

Minorities in the College Classroom: Racism in Education. This 26-minute videotape is designed to sensitize faculty and support staff to cultural differences among students and to help them create a more positive learning environment for both minority and majority students. Eight vignettes illustrate interactions between faculty members and students, showing how faculty–student interaction can enhance or interfere with a minority student's ability to have a successful college experience. The videotape comes with a manual that includes discussion questions, a transcript of each vignette, and background information. *Copies may be purchased or rented (available in ¾", VHS, or Beta) from the Department of Human Relations, Michigan State University, East Lansing, MI 48824-1046.*

Frontline: A Class Divided. This 57-minute video deals with an Iowa teacher's experiment with her third grade class in the 1960s on experiencing prejudice first-hand. The film reviews the original classroom activities, and interviews the participants and the teacher 20 years later. It examines questions of how to change attitudes and behaviors as well as how to

teach about racism and prejudice. Printed materials are also available for classroom use.
CONTACT: *PBS Video, (800) 344-3337.*

Frontline: Racism 101. This 58-minute video reports on incidents of racially motivated violence and harassment on several campuses. Interviews are conducted with students and faculty, surfacing difficult issues concerning racism, prejudice, and individual rights.
CONTACT: *PBS Video, (800) 344-3337.*

8

Teaching, Learning, and the Curriculum

This chapter takes us to the heart of the matter: what happens in the classroom—the interactions between teachers and students, the curriculum, pedagogy, human relationships—is the core of the academic experience.

The following pages deal with complex institutional issues as well as with individual values, attitudes, and behaviors. Because of the complexity of the subject, this chapter will depart from the handbook format; it is more descriptive and analytical in style than prescriptive. It will suggest issues and approaches to consider, rather than strategies to adopt.

Also, few illustrative programs and practices are cited at the end of the chapter. This is so for several reasons. First, much of the chapter deals with interactions between individual teachers and their students; its primary audience is the individual faculty member. Programs to assist faculty improve their teaching are widespread and useful. This *Handbook* cannot attempt to inventory them or review the significant body of work in the area of instructional development. Second, we are in relatively new territory: effective pedagogy is not a new issue, but relating the teaching and learning process to diversity is less familiar. Similarly, we have not had long experience grappling with the issue of whether or how to modify the curriculum to reflect our nation's pluralism.

Finally, the curriculum section draws heavily on the models created by women's studies and feminist scholarship. We do this not to overshadow the importance of racial and ethnic minority issues in the curriculum, but because the paradigms provide helpful conceptual frameworks that are also applicable to minority issues.

We are attempting in this chapter to look at familiar issues in a new light. The emphasis on minority participation to date has been on as-

131

sisting minorities to adapt to the existing norms and practices of the academy. Now we are turning this convention upside down, asking "How should *what* we teach as well as *how* we teach it be changed to reflect a diverse student population and a pluralistic society?" In addition to changing the shape of the proverbial peg, we propose redesigning the hole.

Not for Minorities Only

Quality teaching benefits all students, not just minorities. It is often said that very able students will learn in spite of their teachers, but no faculty member consciously espouses that goal. Certainly, the quality of teaching will make or break academic success for underprepared students, as well as for those who lack study skills or self-confidence—whether they are majority or minority students. And excellent teachers challenge average and able students to new heights.

A curriculum that truly broadens students' horizons and enables them to appreciate different cultures, different modes of thinking and inquiry, and different values and esthetics will benefit *all* students. Thus, women's studies and ethnic studies do not simply provide an intellectual home for these groups of students and faculty, though that is one important function. They should also serve to inform the entire curriculum, enriching the academic experience for all. The infusion of new perspectives and information into the curriculum should affect all students, and, in a larger sense, the academic community as a whole, not just those majority women and minority men and women who are touched by special courses reflective of their origin, experiences, or culture.

The Role of the Faculty

All roads in this chapter lead to the faculty. Teaching, learning, and the curriculum are the undisputed realm of faculty control. Though teaching may be evaluated by one's peers and/or by students, classroom interactions are largely a private matter between the faculty member and the students. Faculty development can be nurtured, encouraged, rewarded, but it cannot easily be mandated. The same is true of curricular change. Students can clamor for change, administrators can provide grants and other incentives to encourage the development of new courses and the revision of existing ones. But more than in any area described in this *Handbook*, faculty leadership, the receptiveness of individual faculty members to new ideas and their commitment to their continued professional growth are essential to positive change.

TEACHING AND LEARNING

First, a word about definitions. "Teaching and learning" are used very broadly in this chapter, referring to the panoply of interactions between students and teachers, and among students, that cause students to master subject matter, to hone their critical thinking, to develop personally and intellectually. "Teaching and learning" encompass inquiry, pedagogy, educational theory, learning styles and preferences, as well as personal growth and development.

Research in teaching and learning is abundant; ironically, little has been deliberately or systematically incorporated by professors into their classroom teaching. (See Claxton and Murrell, 1987, for an excellent summary of the research.) Thus, many of the points made in the following pages will be obvious to those readers who are knowledgeable about educational theory; for many others, whose disciplinary interests do not take them into this realm, the ideas will be newer.

Effective Teaching for All Students: What do We Know?

Most, but not all, of the issues related to teaching minority students are the same as teaching majority students. The traditional and highly prevalent instructional model of the omniscient teacher lecturing to passive students busily taking notes is losing ground, but has by no means disappeared. Many of our college courses are still primarily lectures, with students occupying a passive role in the learning process. Active involvement, frequent feedback, and understanding of different ways of learning are some of the known ways to increase student learning. Recent national reports such as *Involvement in Learning* (NIE, 1984) and *College: The Undergraduate Experience in America* (Boyer, 1987) called attention to these elements of educational effectiveness. The following summary of good practices is reproduced in its entirety from "Seven Principles for Good Practice in Undergraduate Education" in the *Wingspread Journal* (Chickering and Gamson, 1987). The summary is part of a longer article reprinted from the *AAHE Bulletin*, March 1987. The principles are equally applicable to graduate education and serve as a useful point of departure for the subsequent discussion of teaching minority students.

❏   ❏   ❏   ❏   ❏

Seven Principles for Good Practice in Undergraduate Education

1. Good Practice Encourages Student–Faculty Contact.
Frequent student–faculty contact in and out of classes is the most important factor in student motivation and involvement. Faculty concern helps students get through rough times and keep on working. Knowing a few faculty members well enhances students' intellectual commitment and encourages them to think about their own values and future plans.

2. Good Practice Encourages Cooperation Among Students.
Learning is enhanced when it is more like a team effort than a solo race. Good learning, like good work, is collaborative and social, not competitive and isolated. Working with others often increases involvement in learning. Sharing one's own ideas and responding to others' reactions improves thinking and deepens understanding.

3. Good Practice Encourages Active Learning.
Learning is not a spectator sport. Students do not learn much just sitting in class listening to a teacher, memorizing pre-packaged assignments, and spitting out answers. They must talk about what they are learning, write about it, relate it to past experiences, and apply it to their daily lives. They must make what they learn part of themselves.

4. Good Practice Gives Prompt Feedback.
Knowing what you know and don't know focuses learning. Students need appropriate feedback on performance to benefit from courses. In getting started, students need help in assessing existing knowledge and competence. In classes, students need frequent opportunities to perform and receive suggestions for improvement. At various points during college, and at the end, students need chances to reflect on what they have learned, what they still need to know, and how to assess themselves.

5. Good Practice Emphasizes Time on Task.
Time plus energy equal learning. There is no substitute for time on task. Learning to use one's time well is critical for students and pro-

fessionals alike. Students need help in learning effective time management. Allocating realistic amounts of time means effective learning for students and effective teaching for faculty. How an institution defines time expectations for students, faculty, administrators, and other professional staff can establish the basis for high performance for all.

6. Good Practice Communicates High Expectations.
Expect more and you will get it. High expectations are important for everyone—for the poorly prepared, for those unwilling to exert themselves, and for the bright and well motivated. Expecting students to perform well becomes a self-fulfilling prophecy when teachers and institutions hold high expectations of themselves and make extra efforts.

7. Good Practice Respects Diverse Talents and Ways of Learning.
There are many roads to learning. People bring different talents and styles of learning to college. Brilliant students in the seminar room may be all thumbs in the lab or art studio. Students rich in hands-on experience may not do so well with theory. Students need the opportunity to show their talents and learn in ways that work for them. Then they can be pushed to learning in new ways that do not come so easily.

Faculty Attitudes and Behaviors Toward Minority Students
In a perfect world, every faculty member would apply these principles of good practice to all students. The seventh principle reminds us that real differences exist among students. Thus, faculty would also emphasize or de-emphasize a particular practice according to the individual student's need.

Two countervailing forces make it difficult for professors to put these principles into practice. First, the traditional ways in which most faculty were taught in their own undergraduate and graduate experience are natural and comfortable to emulate. This is not to say that every faculty member is a clone of his or her graduate professor, but rather that there is a natural tendency to perpetuate the traditions we have experienced.

Second, while different treatment of minority students can be caused by overt discrimination, this is far less likely among today's faculty members than are unconscious attitudes and behaviors. The following set of questions concerning teaching minority students should help faculty members become more aware of the subliminal messages they communicate to their students. Since some of these behaviors and attitudes are very subtle, most people will be unaware of their extent. Simply raising the questions here can assist faculty to be more conscious of their behaviors, and, therefore, recognize and seek to change the unproductive ones. Users are encouraged to solicit feedback from colleagues and students on perceptions of their behaviors. Videotaping and reviewing one's own teaching are also recommended.

Readers may be disappointed by having these issues raised without clear guidance on how to modify behaviors. Where possible, the *Handbook* offers suggestions. In many cases, however, there are no clear-cut courses of action. Sometimes, understanding more about the silence of a minority student, or about different attitudes and values concerning eye contact will help interpret the behavior of others and prevent a teacher from jumping to unwarranted conclusions. That is an important outcome in itself.

Questions for faculty on attitudes and behaviors with respect to minority students:

1. What are your expectations of minority students? How do you communicate them? At your institution, is it assumed that minority students are generally less well prepared than majority students? What are your assumptions? What is the reality?

Every faculty member will find a range of talent and ability in a class; that comes as no surprise. But it is easy to make unfounded assumptions about which students are more able than others. Research shows that teachers form expectations on the basis of prior achievement, physical attractiveness, sex, language, socioeconomic status, and race/ethnicity (see Good, 1981; and Brophy and Good, 1984). Thus, instructors sometimes assume that minority students will be grouped at the lower end of the ability continuum, and therefore they will have lower expectations of them. These expectations then become self-fulfilling prophecies so that the students in turn do not perform up to capacity.

2. Have you ever been in a situation in which you made a comment or engaged in a behavior that you thought was perfectly innocuous but was considered sexist or racist by a student? How did you receive feedback about how you were perceived? How did you deal with the situation? What was the effect of this episode on you? On the other person? Do you ever ask for feedback from students specifically on these issues?

Majority individuals may say things or engage in behaviors that they do not perceive as disparaging or racist, although they may be perceived as such by minority students. The student will probably not call the professor's attention to this behavior or engage the faculty member in a conversation that could air their different perceptions. The student may then become silently angry or alienated, and the faculty member will have no idea why. Here is an example. Pemberton (1988) cites the situation of a student whose honors thesis advisor spent an inordinate amount of time asking her about her family and private life, rather than focusing on the academic business at hand. The author analyzes the professor's behavior as motivated by an attempt to show interest in his student and reveal his "own lack of racism." The student's interpretation was that "her life was being ransacked for sociological evidence." She did not complain, for the professor had the reputation of being one of the few on campus willing to work with minority students.

Another example occurs in advising. Faculty members may discourage minority students from pursuing mathematics or the hard sciences because they believe that these disciplines are not the students' forte, or that the student would be more successful in another area. Whatever the faculty member's reasoning, the student may interpret this counsel as the professor's inability to imagine a minority student in an academically difficult area. In other words, the student may feel that this advice is based on the assumption that minority students cannot perform as well as majority students in demanding fields of study.

3. How do you deal with silent students? What assumptions do you make about their abilities and attitudes? Do these assumptions differ for majority and minority students?

Minority students are likely to feel uncomfortable in the classrooms of predominantly white institutions for a variety of reasons. The culture may seem alien or intimidating; the nonverbal cues from peers and teachers may inhibit them. Some minority students may be reluctant to participate in class discussions. In some cultures, the professor is seen as an authority figure, not to be questioned, much less disagreed with. Not surprisingly, faculty members may interpret this lack of participation as lack of interest.

Or, students may fear a critical response when speaking up in class. It is easy to interpret their silence as inability or unwillingness to participate, and come to the false conclusion that these students are not academically up to par or have nothing to contribute. Faculty's active solicitation of their participation in a supportive manner can make a crucial difference for minority students.

4. Do you call on minority students as frequently as majority students? When you call on students in class, how long do you wait for them to respond before going on to the next student? Do you wait the same amount of time for a minority student as for a majority student? Do you interrupt students? Do you interrupt minority students more frequently than majority students? Women more than men?

Research on student-teacher interaction has shown that there are often subtle differences in the way teachers interact with low achievers and high achievers (real and perceived). To the extent that minority students are *actually* underprepared, or simply stereotyped as low achievers, they may be treated differently from other students. For example, faculty may unwittingly communicate lower expectations to minority students by calling on them less frequently, by interrupting or critcizing them more frequently, giving them less time to respond to questions or less feedback, moving along rapidly to the next student after their response, or giving general or insincere praise.

5. Do you sustain eye contact with your students? Do you make eye contact as frequently and for equal periods of time with minority students as with majority students? What is your reaction to students who avoid eye contact with you?

Eye contact can be a tricky issue, with different racial and ethnic norms. Direct and sustained eye contact is valued in majority culture as indicating interest and engagement. It is impossible to generalize about minority cultures, both across different racial and ethnic groups and within them. Hispanic students will have different attitudes and cultural habits depending on whether they are first, second, or third generation in this country. Parents' educational backgrounds are also important variables in the acculturation levels of various minority students. A black student whose parents are professors or physicians will have significant cultural differences from a poor inner-city student.

Here are examples of cultural differences with respect to eye contact. In black families, children are sometimes taught that looking an adult in the eye is a sign of disrespect. (Byers and Byers, 1972). In Hispanic culture, sustained eye contact, especially between men and women of slight acquaintance, may be considered to have sexual overtones.

Simply knowing that some members of some minority groups will avoid sustained eye contact provides little concrete guidance for the classroom instructor. It is impossible for a single instructor to know where each student stands on the continuum of cultural differences with respect to eye contact, touching, or joking. However, this information can increase your knowledge of various responses, help you interpret the behaviors of your students and colleagues, and broaden your repertoire of reactions.

6. How are students seated in your classes? What, if any, relationship is there between where majority and minority students sit and their class participation?

Research on primary grade students indicates that students who are physically closest to the teacher receive more academic and nonacademic attention (Daly and Suite, 1982; Rist 1972.) If minority students are reluctant to sit in the front of the classroom or in a position that will provide easy access to the faculty person, it is useful to encourage them to do so, especially in smaller, discussion classes. Seminar-style roundtables or hollow squares are a useful set-up to ensure that all students are equally positioned vis-á-vis the instructor.

7. When the discussion turns to issues that affect or involve minorities, how do you deal with the dilemma of soliciting the input of minority students without imposing on them the role of "spokesperson for their group"?

Minority students in predominantly white institutions often find themselves in a curious bind. On the one hand they are considered representatives of their group. The fewer members of a particular minority group here are on a campus, the more likely that individuals may be looked upon as the persons who can speak to all black or Hispanic issues. On the other hand, back home in their family or community, their immersion in a white institution may earn them the suspicion of their friends and family. In short, they may live in two worlds, but feel that they belong to neither.

Faculty are also in a bind with respect to their minority students. On the one hand, they will certainly want to actively solicit the views of their minority students on any issue that has special bearing on minorities. On the other, they may realize the difficulty and unfairness of implicitly asking a student to speak for all Hispanics or all Asian-Americans. Singling out minority students to respond to racial or ethnic issues is likely to contribute to their sense of isolation.

A genuinely supportive and open attitude can help minority students feel comfortable in speaking out in class, whether or not the subject deals with issues of special concerns to minorities; it can also ensure that majority students appreciate the viewpoints of all students.

8. How do you give feedback to students? Are there differences between the amount and type of feedback you give to minority and majority students and the manner in which it is delivered?

Feedback is crucial to effective learning. Good feedback goes far beyond grades on tests and papers, and comments in the margin. It requires discussion of the student's work, his or her strengths and weaknesses, and a willingness to speak frankly, being critical if necessary. Positive feedback is the easiest to give and receive, and there is a natural and understandable tendency to avoid giving negative feedback. Minority students, like all other students, need both encouragement and positive feedback; they need constructive criticism as well. If delivered constructively, criticism can help students understand areas in which they need to improve and leave them feeling positive and motivated.

Suggested next steps

Incorporating and acting on the information presented here are not easy. To do so requires being conscious of behaviors we take for granted, and discussing issues with our students and colleagues that are not usually part of our conversations. This new self-consciousness about teaching and learning may seem artificial or strained. But that is the only way we know how to incorporate important and useful knowledge about teaching and learning into our everyday academic lives.

1. In work groups (department meetings, department chair or deans' meetings, or in a task force), discuss the questions listed above and add any items you deem useful. Seek input from resource people who are knowledgeable in fields such as learning theory, educational psychology, cognitive development, communications, multicultural education.

2. Have regular sessions with minority students to assess their perceptions of the classroom culture. Make these open sessions, where both students and faculty are learners. Try to act on the points they raise and begin the process again.

Learning Styles and Minority Students

One of the "Principles of Good Practice" emphasizes the need to respect diverse talents and ways of learning. Learning theory is not new, and it is well established that individuals learn differently. The term "learning style" is sometimes used differently by different individuals. In this *Handbook*, we use it broadly, to include how people process and retain information, how they prefer to interact with teachers and other learners, and what kind of learning environment they prefer.

Learning style and gender, race, and ethnicity

The relationship of gender, racial, and ethnic differences to learning styles presents a double controversy. First, is it even legitimate to identify certain learning styles with gender, race, or ethnicity? For some, the answer is *no*. In 1987, the New York State Board of Regents recommended that teachers become more aware of how different cultural backgrounds affect communication and learning. This recommendation turned into a bitter debate about the appropriateness of generalizing about racial and ethnic groups. A recent *Harvard Education Letter* on "Cultural Differences in the Classroom" commented:

> Most educators agree that students approach learning in many different ways and that teachers need to take these differences into account in developing their instructional strategies. But no consensus exists as to *which* differences matter in terms of learning. There is, in fact, active disagreement as to whether the cultural backgrounds of students should be singled out for attention.

The danger, of course, is stereotyping. The dilemma lies in recognizing diversity, even when it breaks along gender or racial/ethnic lines, without casting all members of a group into the same stereotypical mold. In spite of the objections of those who claim that to generalize is to stereotype, research does indicate that there is some relationship between culture, conceptual systems, and learning styles (Claxton and Murrell, 1987; Anderson, 1988). Perceptual and cognitive differences have been demonstrated between different minority groups and Euro-Americans. In U.S. culture, not surprisingly, the male-oriented Euro-American style is the dominant one, and therefore the most highly valued in education.

The second point of controversy turns on the "why" of differences in learning style: the familiar nature/nurture question. Most, but not all, researchers maintain that gender or race may influence preferred learning style because the style is either valued or reinforced by that group or by the majority culture. For example, the perception that women are often collaborative rather than competitive learners may be attributable to the fact that the dominant culture rewards and reinforces those tendencies in women and discourages them in men. Similarly, Hale-Benson's (1982) research shows that black children tend to be more relational than analytical in their learning styles, but, as most instructors know, these differences may be minimized or disappear altogether when students are acculturated to the predominant analytic style of most schools.

Much of the resistance to the issue of culturally based learning styles stems from the implicit assumption that what differs from the norm is less valuable. Therefore, some minority persons object to research findings that nonwhite groups have a learning style that relies more on synthesis than analysis. It is useful to view learning styles as a question of preference rather than of absolutes, and to recognize that students need opportunities to exercise their preferred style as well as develop their weaker styles.

A conceptual framework for a continuum of learning styles

This *Handbook* cannot resolve these continuing dilemmas. It can, however, help you think through the issues by presenting a schema that describes a continuum of learning styles. Use it to examine how your students learn, to note differences among your students by age, gender, race, and ethnicity.

Remember that the schema represents a continuum, with most majority and minority students falling somewhere between the two extreme ends. Also, the level of generality of the schema makes it only a point of departure for discussion; no one is "pure type" in any category.

The characteristics described on the left side of the schema represent one pole in the models described above (personality, information processing, social interaction, instructional preference). These characteristics are more frequently ascribed to women and members of minority groups. Since learning styles are *preferences*, however, it is important to remember that learners will shift from one style to another and the predominant style can change over time.

Learning style and teaching style

The obvious question that comes to mind at this point is, "What are the practical consequences of this information?" Certainly, no faculty member can adapt his or her teaching to the individual needs of every learner in the class. Does this information, then, fall into the

Table 5: A Continuum of Learning Styles

Field-dependent Relational/holistic Affective	Field-independent Analytic Nonaffective
Characteristics	Characteristics
1. Perceive elements as part of a total picture.	1. Perceive elements as discrete from their background.
2. Do best on verbal tasks.	2. Do best on analytic tasks.
3. Learn material that has a human social content and that is characterized by fantasy and humor.	3. Learn material that is inanimate and impersonal more easily.
4. Performance influenced by authorizing figure's expression of confidence or doubt.	4. Performance not greatly affected by the opinions of others.
5. Style conflicts with traditional school environment.	5. Style matches most school environments.

Based on James A. Anderson, "Cognitive Styles and Multicultural Populations," *Journal of Teacher Education,* January/February 1988, table 2, p. 6.

category of "interesting to know" but "not very helpful in the classroom"? It need not. Once again, principles of effective teaching and a dose of common sense can be helpful. We know that variety in the classroom—in the styles of presentation, of the types of assignments that students receive, will help different students shine in different circumstances. For some, mastery of facts will be a strong suit; for others, it will be interpreting the material and spinning out new ideas. Learning activities that involve the factual and the imaginative, the affective and the cognitive, independent and collaborative work, will enable students to exercise their strengths as well as shore up their nonpreferred styles.

Using learning style to help students learn

An understanding of the range of possible learning styles and one's own preferences can help students feel more confident about learning as well as use their strengths to their advantage. Claxton and Murrell (1987) describe efforts at two community colleges to institutionalize the use of cognitive mapping to help students understand their style, select courses consistent with the style, and develop strategies for academic success (p. 50). Mt. Hood Community College is one of a number of colleges that requires a one-hour course in psychology titled "College and Career Planning," which helps students understand their learning styles as well as provides career information.

The opportunity to learn about one's own learning style and the options for different learning strategies could make a big difference for all students; it could be a crucial intervention for students who learn differently from the "norm."

Also, students can actively seek to broaden their repertoire of learning styles. Learning resource centers and new forms of computer-assisted instruction can assist learners to transcend different teaching styles and learn effectively. For example, a computer program to help students study biology was introduced at the University of Michigan with demonstrable results in the achievement levels of minority students. (Kleinsmith, 1987). Courses teaching students how to learn, such as "Learning to Learn Instructional Course," have had success in improving GPAs and retention rates.

Strategies for faculty

1. Take a learning style inventory and discuss it in department, faculty, or committee meeting. (One widely used inventory is the *Learning Style Inventory* by David Kolb, 1976, available from McBer and Co, Boston, MA.) Use an expert as a resource. Discuss the implications of your own learning style for how you teach and how you learn. Discuss the implications of the various learning styles people have for departmental offerings, faculty evaluation methods, graduate training, future research.

2. Administer a learning style inventory to students with the help of an expert. Discuss the implications of their learning style for your course and your teaching style.

3. Develop programs designed to assist students understand their learning styles and to learn how to learn.

Strategies for administrators

1. Sponsor professional development programs to help faculty understand issues of learning style, teaching style, and their role in improving student learning.

2. Offer minigrants to faculty to promote research to help understand diverse learning styles and adaptation of teaching styles and course materials to these different styles.

THE CURRICULUM

Issues surrounding the curriculum have always generated a great deal of disagreement. Opponents of "modern" works in the curriculum touted the classics as the true path to education; advocates of professionalism battled defenders of the liberal arts; and academics have continually debated the form and content of the core curriculum.

In spite of the controversies generated by the curriculum, a general consensus does exist concerning the overall purposes of a liberal education. Phrases such as "an appreciation of history, science, and artistic traditions," "fostering ethical conduct," and "synthesis of knowledge" abound in discussions of undergraduate education. The general principles are familiar territory; the interpretation and relative importance of each as well as the curricular paths to implementation are not.

It is also widely agreed that the curriculum is not static; faculties are constantly re-examining and revising it to reflect new knowledge and the changing conditions and requirements of the society. Curriculum changes in two ways: one is through the addition of new knowledge, and the second is through reconsidering and re-evaluating existing knowledge. Curriculum change may be effected by faculty members who develop new expertise or by the addition of new faculty who bring different perspectives and academic training.

There are numerous examples of new knowledge affecting the curriculum that are both familiar to, and prized by, the academy. New knowledge is created all the time in the sciences. It is both *added* to the curriculum, and in addition frequently causes a *re-examination* and *recasting* of existing theories and facts. Sometimes new information renders existing theories or "facts" totally invalid.

Here are some simplified examples. Computer science has not only created a new discipline, but has also reshaped teaching in other fields. Being "computer literate" is often incorporated in definitions of liberally educated persons. In the realm of scientific discovery, new knowledge reshapes old knowledge and theories. The discovery that the world was round not only disproved the notion that the world was flat, but also invalidated other theories and practices based on that concept. The discovery of DNA resulted in the addition of new concepts to the field of genetics; these concepts were reflected in new material in biology, chemistry, and genetics textbooks. Furthermore, the discovery of DNA caused previous research to be re-evaluated in a new light. Another example is found in the humanities. In literary scholarship, the development of new critical theories such as deconstructionism gave scholars both a new set of literary theories (new information) as well as new ways to approach classical texts (re-examination).

Clearly, the last 25 years have brought profound changes to colleges and universities. The increased number of women students, minority men students, and older students have transformed student bodies. New areas of knowledge, new disciplines, and new educational issues have emerged. Afro-American studies, American studies, American ethnic studies, area studies, women's studies, and interdisciplinary studies were created to respond to the growing recognition that college and university curricula were omitting the experiences and contributions of large segments of our society. Thus, they were providing an incomplete and unidimensional education. Institutions are responding to this challenge by offering freshman seminars on issues of gender and race, or by requiring a course in world civilization that includes Western civilization, or by requiring one in Third World culture.

The journey has not been an easy one. Controversy still plagues ethnic studies and women's studies. For example, the debate continues as to whether Afro-American studies is a legitimate discipline (Huggins, 1985, p. 55). The question of whether women's studies and Afro-American studies should stand as separate programs is still debated. Opponents of separate departments or programs argue that their importance is not necessarily measured by the existence of a separate department and that these subjects should be part of the "regular curriculum."

Afro-American studies, ethnic studies, and women's studies have made contributions to scholarship that have found their way into the curriculum through the processes we have just discussed. These programs have recovered and clarified past history, and have also challenged the certainties we have held about human behavior. Much of the literature on this change process has been developed in the field of women's studies. The 20 years of scholarship and debate in this field shed a great deal of light on our present discussion.

Feminist scholars make the point that the contribution of women's studies is not only adding a new body of knowledge about half the world's population, but also pointing to "reconceptualizations of knowledge itself, of education, and of societal structures. . . ." This new scholarship "provides a systematic way to critique our present systems and clarify the ways these systems operate to exclude many people" (McIntosh, forthcoming, p. 2). Feminist scholarship has also been enriched by black women's studies, which have pointed out the dangers of overgeneralizing about any one group. Black women scholars have further refined the discussion to point out the crucial intersection of race, class, and gender as filters for experience.

The discussion that follows draws on the concepts developed in women's studies. These concepts can be expanded and modified to shed light on the development of new knowledge and the re-examination of existing knowledge from the perspective of racial and ethnic minorities.

Transforming the Curriculum: the Current Debate

The current national debate over the curriculum centers on whether or how to make the curriculum reflective of the cultural plurality that characterizes the U.S. and the world. The movement to "transform" the curriculum aims to ensure that majority and minority students understand the rich history, art, and literature of women and ethnic and racial minorities, that they analyze the unstated assumptions and perspectives that underlie scholarship, and that American culture be placed in a broad global context.

The recent debate at Stanford University has had high visibility, but many campuses across the country are also struggling with this issue. The national dialogue about the transformation of the curriculum is still in its early stages. It is marked by profound philosophical and value differences. The emotionally charged part of the debate centers on the inclusion of works and perspectives of minorities and women. This inclusion is not proposed simply as an "add on," but as a force that will transform the entire teaching and learning process. It is a long-term proposition. Another related but less controversial thread in the curricular debate deals with "internationalizing the curriculum," that is, weaving through the curriculum the reality of a multicultural interdependent world. The efforts to make the curriculum more pluralistic and more international have the common goal of increasing students' (and faculty's) awareness of the richness and complexity of knowledge.

Critics of the status quo contend that the standard curriculum is anchored in a male centered, Anglo-European perspective, ignoring the history and contributions of large segments of our population and riddled with perceptual bias that devalues non Anglo-European subjects or approaches to learning. Some critics claim that the current male, Eurocentric emphasis of the curriculum reflects "institutional racism." Others, less concerned with the origin of the problem than with its consequences, contend that the current curriculum leaves little room for understanding different points of view and different cultures, and that it keeps minorities and women marginal to the academic experience. In addition, the current curriculum does not expose the "invisible paradigms" which are "the internalized assumptions, the network of unspoken agreements, the implicit contracts that all the participants in the process of higher education have agreed to, unusually unconsciously, in order to bring about learning" (Schuster and Van Dyne, 1984, p. 417).

Defenders of the existing curriculum maintain that transforming the curriculum represents an attempt to introduce political viewpoints into a neutral curriculum. They claim that the proponents of a transformed curriculum seek to distort it with their own politically motivated reform agendas. *Washington Post* writer Jonathan Yardley wrote, "Who cares about the facts when the real game being played has nothing to do with literature and everything to do with retrograde '60s politics and academic careerism?" Another defender of the traditional curriculum, Gertrude Himmelfarb, commented in the *New York Times* that (1988) "it used to be thought that ideas transcend race, gender and class, that there are such things as truth, reason, morality and artistic excellence, which can be understood and aspired to by everyone, of whatever race, gender or class." There is room in the current curriculum to examine all these issues, and free inquiry will surface them without forcing "the new academic shibboleth" on students.

Transforming the curriculum is no more political than the process that designates the existing "canon," claims Henry Louis Gates, Jr., professor at Cornell University (1988):

> That people can maintain a straight face while they protest the eruption of politics into something that has always been political from the very beginning says something about how remarkably successful official literary histories have been at disguising all linkages between the canon, the literary past we remember, and those interests that maintain it.

Perhaps a more promising approach to this debate is to frame it in terms of an inclusionary change process. This reframing moves the discussion away from the polarities of political vs. the "value neutral," the old or the new, and permits dialogue and debate on curricular change and incorporating new visions without sacrificing what is valuable in the existing curriculum.

Taking Action on Your Campus: A Framework for Transforming the Curriculum

To some extent, the debate on *whether* to transform the curriculum is unnecessary, for there is already a significant new body of scholarship on ethnic studies and women's studies as well as new epistemologies resulting from this scholarship. The movement to transform the curriculum is growing. New kinds of scholarship are engaging a wide spectrum of academics and others in debate, and clearly are exerting an influence on what we teach and how we teach it. It is increasingly difficult to ignore the new scholarship and its proponents. The question that faces us now is how widely their influence will be felt. Will it remain separate and marginal to the rest of scholarly inquiry and teaching, or will its influence permeate the campus?

This *Handbook* takes the position that the curriculum must change over time. Knowledge and scholarship are not neutral, and the constant examination of assumptions, values, and biases in the curriculum is a desirable and inevitable process. New scholarship cannot be excluded from the curriculum.

Phases of Transforming the Curriculum

Higher education is already in the midst of an evolutionary process. The following framework for considering the course of change is adapted from Peggy McIntosh (1983 and forthcoming) and Schuster and Van Dyne (1984). Useful discussions of integrating Afro-American history in the curriculum are Griffin (1979) and Huggins (1986).

Phase 1: *The Exclusive Curriculum.* This phase excludes the works and perspectives of non-Western cultures and of minorities and women. Such a curriculum does not include courses or programs in Afro-American studies, ethnic studies, or women's studies. The criteria of greatness used to select the great thinkers and actors in history are embedded in the unexamined "invisible paradigm." It is not perceived as exclusionary, but rather as searching for greatness that transcends time, place, gender, and culture. This phase typifies the pre-1960s curriculum.

Phase 2: *The Exceptional Outsider.* In this phase, a few superstar minority or female figures might be studied in a course, but, as McIntosh puts it, this phase "does not challenge the traditional outlines and winner-focused definitions of those who 'made' history" (forthcoming, p. 17). Thus, W.E. DuBois might be included in a course on American intellectual history, or Scott Momaday in a contemporary fiction course, but they remain exceptional and do not fundamentally change the way we look at literature or history. The exceptional outsiders (majority and minority women and minority men) are measured by the predominant male model.

Phase 3: *Understanding the Outsider.* At this point, special courses may be introduced into the curriculum to analyze and understand excluded groups. The curriculum raises the questions of why there are so few minority leaders, and why their traditional roles are devalued. While the importance of the outsider is acknowledged in this phase, it is still in the mode of "otherness," for the really important figures and ideas continue to be the ones who have traditionally dominated the curriculum. A course on black American authors may (but not necessarily) focus on their art as secondary to, or growing out of, the literary canon formed by white writers. Thus, the focus remains on understanding the outsider, rather than revisiting the canon that has established the rules as to who is outside and what is "mainstream." This phase is likely to produce anger as comfortable structures are pulled apart and the "invisible paradigms" exposed.

Phase 4: *Getting Inside the Outsider:* Now, the perspective switches from that of the dominant group to that of the outsider. "Reality" is seen from many perspectives, and the multiple nature of that reality becomes clear. For example, in literature the narrative voice of slaves or American Indians may portray the world through their eyes, using their voices and constructs, rather than depicting them as they are seen by whites.

Phase 5: *The Transformed Curriculum.* Here, the curriculum takes very seriously the question of what were the perspectives and experiences of non-Western civilizations, of women, of minority groups, of those who made history but were not the "giants" that we have traditionally studied. The curriculum in this new state is transformed in four distinct and intertwined ways:

First, **it incorporates new knowledge and new scholarship.** The transformed curriculum does not simply add a course on women here, or one on Hispanic culture there; it imagines new ways to organize and arrange knowledge. It self-consciously examines the "invisible paradigm" and offers alternatives. It asks new questions such as, "What was going on in the rest of the world while x was happening in the U.S.?" "How would my discipline need to change to reflect the experiences of minorities, or other cultures?" "What was happening to farmers, laborers, children during the 'great events' of history we are examining?" What basic assumptions about science would be different if new perspectives were used?

Second, **it incorporates new methodologies**—the letters of great men stand alongside diaries of farmers, slaves, and pioneer women, county records and oral histories as testimonies of an historical era.

Third, a transformed curriculum **encourages new ways of thinking**, of posing the fundamental epistemological questions "How do we know what we know?" "How do we know what we are excluding?" "What are the assumptions that underlie the 'objective' questions we traditionally pose?" New theories or paradigms are needed to explain knowledge, since, when new knowledge comes to light, the old paradigms may not be adequate to interpret it. The new curriculum allows for subjective ways of knowing as well as the generally accepted "objective" ways. New implications of "subjective" and "objective" would be explored which would cast them in terms that would no longer make the latter more desirable than the former.

Fourth, **it incorporates new ways of teaching and learning** that acknowledge collaborative as well as individual learning. Parker J. Palmer (1987) makes the point that the prevailing epistemology in higher education assumes that the individual "is the agent of knowing" and that learning is therefore objective and analytical. He argues that, because learning is a communal activity, dependent on a lively exchange of ideas and conflict, our current epistemology does not serve us well. Recognition of a communal way of knowing, he continues, will allow higher education to combine objectivity and intimacy or personal identification with the subject matter, not to be forced to choose between the "'hard' virtues of cognition against the 'soft' virtues of community" (p. 25).

Conclusion: Creating a Win/Win Curriculum and Learning Environment

Too much of the current debate on the curriculum is posed as an either/or situation. Either we cling to the canon or adopt the new scholarship; either we remain value-neutral or politicize the curriculum; either we become ossified or radical. In the arena of teaching and learning, we imagine choosing between collaborative learning and solitary scholarship, between learners who are logical and abstract and those who are concrete and relational.

Out of this dialectic there may emerge a middle course, one that will preserve elements of the curriculum and some teaching practices, and revise others. That middle course will not force faculties to choose between teaching Shakespeare and Alice Walker. The academic values that should be incorporated in a transformed curriculum are ones that every professor could easily espouse: there are many truths and many roads to those truths; the curriculum is not engraved in stone and it will continue to evolve as our society evolves; no discipline and no mode of inquiry is intrinsically more meritorious than another—each fills different and legitimate purposes.

The point here is that to exclude a variety of modes of teaching, learning, or inquiry, or bodies of knowledge is to shortchange everyone. We live in an information society and our institutions of higher learning should by definition reflect that.

Recommendations for Action

The next steps are still of a preliminary nature. Many, if not most, institutions have not yet immersed themselves in discussions of transforming the curriculum. Some, such as Towson State University and Hartwick College, are taking steps to integrate women's studies throughout the curriculum; others such as Brown University and the New Jersey Department of Education are providing grants to faculty to revise their courses to be more inclusive of women and minorities. For most institutions, the process can begin by opening the dialogue. Below is a list of discussion questions to assist in that process.

Checklist of Discussion Questions

1. What are our current offerings in Afro-American studies? ethnic studies? women's studies? Are they separate programs, departments? Profile their enrollments. Which courses have higher/lower enrollment? What is the composition of the student body who enrolls in these courses? (To what extent are majority and minority men taking women's studies courses? To what extent are majority men and women taking ethnic studies courses?) What is the prevailing campus attitude about these courses?

2. Are there any requirements in place that ensure that students develop a familiarity with ethnic and minority studies and culture and history? If not, should there be?

3. How are faculty encouraged to incorporate new perspectives into their courses? Is there provision for release time? stipends to support research? grants for new course development?

4. Are faculty encouraged to increase their knowledge of different learning styles and teaching styles? Do you offer workshops, semi-

nars, or minigrants to assist faculty in improving their teaching
and in understanding issues related to teaching in a pluralistic environment? How else might faculty be assisted in improving teaching?

5. Are faculty efforts to transform the curriculum or to improve
teaching awarded in promotion, tenure, merit pay? Should they
be? If so, how?

PROGRAMS AND PRACTICES

Odyssey II, Brown University Program. Brown has embarked on a
three-year program, sponsored jointly by the university and by a
$250,000 grant from the Ford Foundation, in which teams of under-
graduate students and faculty work together to supplement course
lectures and reading lists and to create new courses. Grants are
awarded to students to enable them to work with professors and reference librarians to develop new bibliographies and sources; the
grants also provide release time for faculty members. A number of
the collaborative projects are focused on incorporating new racial or
ethnic perspectives in the curriculum. The project aims to interest
students in college teaching as a career as well as to create a mechanism to feed new ideas into Brown's course offerings. In its first year,
the program funded 88 research collaborations, approximately 30 of
which focused on racial and ethnic diversity.
**Contact Karen T. Romer, Associate Dean, College of Arts and Sci-
ences, Brown University, (401) 863-4221.**

**New Jersey Department of Higher Education Competitive Grant Pro-
gram.** The Department offers competitive grants open to all faculty
of the 56 public institutions in the state. The humanities grant program, a $1.3 million dollar grant program, and the international and
foreign language grant program, awarding $420,000, encourage proj-
ects that incorporate gender and multicultural perspectives.
**Contact: Judy Himes, New Jersey Department of Higher Education,
(609) 292-9044.**

The New Jersey Project: Integrating the Scholarship on Gender. The
New Jersey Department of Higher Education will give $362,500 over
three years to support the work of faculty members of 56 colleges in
revising their courses to reflect a more balanced view of women and
minorities. The funds support changes in courses as well as special
workshops and collaboration among faculty members on different
campuses. A summer institute includes teams from many institutions (the 1988 workshop included 14) to discuss the strategies and

processes of change as well as new scholarship. One-day conferences are held throughout the year. A similar project on integrating multicultural perspectives in the curriculum is in the planning phase. **Contact: Judy Himes, New Jersey Department of Education, (609) 292-9044, or Carol Smith, Director, Institute for Research on Women, Rutgers University, (201) 932-9072.**

"A New Approach: Promoting Articulation and Transfer in the Community College," League for the Humanities. In 1987 the League received a $250,000 grant from the Ford Foundation for this project. The Ford grant provided $25,000 grants to six community colleges to assist them in undertaking curriculum revision that will facilitate transfer. The revisions will emphasize the humanities curricula and nontraditional students—part-time, minority, women, adults, and first-generation college goers. Six community colleges were selected to participate through a national competition: Los Medanos College, CA; Metropolitan Community Colleges, MS; Oakton Community College, IL; Phoenix College, AZ; Pima Community College, AZ; Tacoma Community College, WA. Each developed a cooperative plan with baccalaureate institutions to create an Institute for Curricular Redesign. The campus-based institutes bring together faculty and administrators from the participating institutions to redesign, introduce, and create new integrated sequences in the humanities curricula to overcome traditional barriers to student transfer. **Contact: Len Oliver, Executive Director, League for the Humanities, (202) 362-1522.**

Mathematics Workshop Program, University of California at Berkeley. The Mathematics Workshop grew out of the research of Uri Treisman on the academic difficulties experienced by black students in mathematics courses. Formally launched in 1978 with 42 students and two part-time staff members, students met for two hours a day, three or four days a week, led by staff with graduate training in mathematics and demonstrated excellence in teaching. The workshops are not remedial; students work for a grade of B or better in calculus or chemistry (added to the program later). Collaborative learning and small-group teaching methods are stressed. In addition to the solid academic base, students can receive knowledgeable and sympathetic academic or personal counseling and obtain aid in navigating the university's bureaucracy.

Between 1979 and 1985, 55 percent of the workshop's 231 black students (compared with 21 percent of the 234 black students not in the workshop) had earned a B- or better in first year calculus. Two-thirds of the black workshop students graduated from the university; fewer than half of non-workshop black students did. Since 1988, the work-shops are conducted as part of the regular instruction and are known as "intensive/honors" sections of freshman calculus. Sections are open to all students but minority students are specially recruited and constitute approximately one-half to two-thirds of the section enrollment.

Contact: Uri Treisman, Professional Development Program, 230-B Stephens Hall, University of California at Berkeley, Berkeley, CA 94720, (415) 642-2115.

Resources

An Inclusive Curriculum: Race Class, and Gender in Sociological In-struction, **Patricia Hill Collins and Margeret L. Andersen, eds. A joint project of the American Sociological Association Teaching Center, the Section on Racial and Ethnic Minorities, and the Section on Sex and Gender. Washington D.C. American Sociological Association, 1987.**
The Sourcebook begins with several essays establishing a conceptual framework for integrating issues of race, class, and gender in the cur-riculum. The majority of the book is devoted to detailed descriptions and syllabi of courses specifically on the topic of race, sex, and class, or general sociology courses incorporating these perspectives.

Contact: ASA Teaching Resources Center, 1722 N Street, N.W., Washington, D.C. 20034, (202) 833-3410.

REFERENCES

Andersen, James A. 1988. "Cognitive Styles and Multicultural Populations." *Journal of Teacher Education*, Jan/Feb, pp. 2-9.

Boyer, Ernest L. 1987. *College: The Undergraduate Experience in America.* New York: Harper & Row. 1984.

Brophy, J.E., and T.L. Good. 1984. *Teacher Behavior and Student Achievement. Occasional Paper No. 73.* Bethesda, MD: ERIC Document Reproductions Service ED 251 422.

Byers, P., and H. Byers. 1972. "Nonverbal communication and the education of children." In C.B. Cazden, V.P. John, and D. Hynes (eds.), *Functions of language in the classroom.* New York: Academic Press, 1972. Cited by R.S. Feldman. "Nonverbal Behavior, Race and the Classroom Teacher." *Theory into Practice* (24) Winter 1985, pp. 455-49.

Chickering, Arthur W., and Zelda F. Gamson. 1987. "Seven Principles for Good Practice in Undergraduate Education." Special insert to the *Wingspread Journal*, vol. 9, no. 2, published by the Johnson Foundation, P.O. Box 547, Racine, Wisconsin 53401-0547.

Claxton, Charles S., and Patricia H. Murrell, eds. 1987. *Learning Styles: Implications for Improving Educational Practices.* ASHE-ERIC Higher Education Report No. 4. Washington, D.C.: Association for the Study of Higher Education.

Daly, J., and A. Suite. 1981–82. "Classroom Seating Choice and Teacher Perceptions of Students." *Journal of Experimental Education* (50) Winter 1981–82, pp. 64–69.

Curry, L. 1983. "An Organization of Learning Styles Theory and Constructs." Paper presented at the annual meeting of the American Educational Research Association, Montreal, Quebec, April. ED 235 185, 22 pp.

Furmann, Barbara, and Anthony Grasha. 1983. *Designing Classroom Experiences Based on Student Styles and Teaching Styles: A Practical Handbook for College Teaching.* Boston: Little, Brown.

Gates, Henry Louis. 1988. In "Setting the Standards for Literary Masterpieces." *New York Times,* May 29.

Good, Thomas L. 1981. "Teacher Expectations and Student Perceptions: A Decade of Research." *Educational Leadership,* February, pp. 417–422.

Griffin, Everett. 1979. *The Politics of Education.* Chicago: Adams Press.

Hale-Benson, Janice E. 1982. *Black Children: Their Roots, Culture and Learning Styles.* Baltimore: John Hopkins University Press.

Himmelfarb, Gertrude. 1988. "Stanford and Duke Undercut Classical Values." *New York Times,* May 5.

Huggins, Nathan I. 1986. "Integrating Afro-American History into American History." In Darlene C. Hine (ed.), *The State of Afro-American History, Past Present and Future.* Baton Rouge, Louisiana State University Press.

Kleinsmith, Lewis J. 1987. "A Computer-Based Biology Study Center." *Academic Computing,* vol. 2, no. 3, pp. 32–33.

Kolb, David A. 1976. *Learning Style Inventory.* Boston: McBer.

McIntosh, Peggy. Forthcoming. "Curricular Re-Vision: The New Knowledge for a New Age." In Carol Pearson, Judith Touchton, and Donna Shavlik (eds.), *Educating the*

Majority: Women Challenge Tradition in Higher Education. New York: American Council on Education/Macmillan Publishing Co.

———. 1983. *Interactive Phases of Curricular Re-vision: A Feminist Perspective,* working paper no. 124. Wellesley, MA: Wellesley College Center for Research on Women.

National Institute of Education (NIE). 1984. *Involvement in Learning: Realizing the Potential of American Higher Education.* Washington DC: U.S. Government Printing Office.

Palmer, Parker J. 1987. "Community, Conflict, and Ways of Knowing: Ways to Deepen our Educational Agenda." *Change*, September/October, pp. 20–25.

Pemberton, Gayle. 1988. *On Teaching the Minority Students: Problems and Strategies.* Brunswick, ME: Bowdoin College.

Rist, R. 1972. "Social Distance and Social Inequality in a Ghetto Kindergarten Classroom." *Urban Education* (7), October, pp. 241–60.

Schuster, Marilyn, and Susan Van Dyne. 1984. "Placing Women in the Liberal Arts: Stages of Curriculum Transformation." *Harvard Educational Review*, vol. 54, no. 4, November, pp. 413–28.

9

Three Institutions Making a Difference:

The University of Massachusetts at Boston; Miami-Dade Community College; Mount St. Mary's College

Institutional leaders who have made serious and sustained efforts to increase minority participation are the first to recognize the work that remains to be done on their own campuses. There are no perfect models, but there are success stories. The colleges and universities described here, the University of Massachusetts at Boston, Miami-Dade Community College, and Mount St. Mary's College, are examples of institutions that have undertaken comprehensive, institution-wide efforts to make their campuses hospitable and supportive environments for minority students, faculty, and administrators. As the institutional profiles that follow describe, the efforts of the three schools have several common elements: leadership from the top, sustained support for students, and a commitment to institutional change and to diversity as part of the campus ethos.

The lessons from these diverse institutions—public, private, two-year and four-year—are useful. Certainly, these three urban campuses enjoy the advantage of proximity to minority populations, which is certainly not the case for all campuses. Nonetheless, their experiences are instructive, their accomplishments inspiring.

❏   ❏   ❏   ❏   ❏

The University of Massachusetts at Boston

T he University of Massachusetts at Boston demonstrates how senior leadership and broad-based commitment can make minority presence on campus a fundamental institutional value. At the end of the 1970s, amidst city-wide attention to racial conflict, a new chancellor, Robert Corrigan, made minority presence a primary leadership issue. Both on the campus and in the broader Boston community, the chancellor set a tone for the university by giving particular and sustained attention to activities affecting minority participation in education, business, and community development.

BACKGROUND: A CLIMATE FOR CHANGE

The University of Massachusetts at Boston was founded in 1965 as the urban campus of the state's public land-grant university. By the late '70s, after a period of rapid growth, UMass/Boston's rate of expansion had slowed. The faculty was not increasing substantially and many departments were highly tenured. Graduate programs had not developed as expected. Frequent changes in administrative leadership had left the campus uncertain about its direction in several areas. In particular, affirmative action and minority recruitment were not at the top of the institution's agenda, though its policies called for a diverse student body.

In the city, racial tension was high. The public schools operated under the mandate of a U.S. District Court, and busing had been in effect for five years. Racial issues dominated the news and the community atmosphere. Business, political, and community leaders were approaching consensus that major initiatives were needed to solve the crisis. Nevertheless, no specific programs had emerged.

Robert Corrigan was appointed chancellor of the Boston campus in 1979. He became an active and visible participant in shaping the agenda of both the city and the university to confront racial issues. Inside the university, the chancellor and the affirmative action office forged a close partnership.

RECRUITING FACULTY, STAFF, AND ADMINISTRATORS

Procedures

A new set of procedures transformed the affirmative action plan from a compliance-oriented manual into a set of results-oriented action items. The policy now requires that the Affirmative Action Office, led by experienced black professionals, approve all searches in the university—whether faculty, professional staff, or classified—at three stages: (1) approval of the job description and advertisement before recruitment; (2) approval of the applicant pool before selection of the finalists; and (3) approval of the recommended appointee. Disapproval at any stage by the Affirmative Action Office requires revision or repetition of the process.

The affirmative action officer's review has several primary concerns. The job descriptions and ads must be nondiscriminatory. Recommended salary ranges must be competitive enough to attract well-qualified minority applicants. Finally, national representation of minorities in various academic disciplines or professions must be the minimum benchmark for UMass/Boston departments. If recommended appointments do not help departments accomplish minority and female employment goals, they can be disapproved. Disapproval of the final recommendation for appointment can be overturned only by personal action of the chancellor. Individual department heads are held accountable through their annual performance reviews for success in meeting affirmative action procedures and goals.

Outreach

The Affirmative Action Office publishes a recruitment brochure specifically addressed to minority faculty and staff. The brochure emphasizes the institution's commitment to minority presence, focusing on current staff, organizations, and procedures. The affirmative action officer is supported by the university in offering a series of affirmative action workshops for personnel experts in Boston agencies, business, and colleges in order to improve their procedures and techniques in minority recruitment. The university has thus become a resource to Boston organizations in the recruitment of minorities.

Recruitment Incentives and Funding

The chancellor and dean of the College of Arts and Sciences collaborated on a minority faculty recruitment incentive program. It offered new faculty positions to departments with comparatively low minority representation. Even if other planning criteria would not justify new hires, departments could compete for positions by recruiting and appointing excellently qualified minority candidates. The institution recognizes that it needs competitive salaries for minority recruitment just as in the recruitment of other professionals in high-demand disciplines.

RECRUITMENT AND RETENTION OF MINORITY STUDENTS

When Boston State College closed in 1982, the minority community feared that access to four-year college programs would suffer. But the university affirmed its commitment to the minority population in several ways. In the Office of Enrollment Services, minority recruitment was reaffirmed and emphasized. The Developmental Studies Program—an existing summer program for inner-city students with weak academic preparation—was increased by 50 percent. The university has increased its focus on high school tracks leading to college entry through programs like "Urban Scholars" and "Another Course to College." The Urban Scholars Program reaches 250 academically promising students from middle and high schools. It provides students with curricular and counseling support, including thorough exposure to the university and university life. Thus far, 99 percent of the students in the Urban Scholars Program have gone on to college, at UMass/Boston or other institutions.

A PLURALISTIC CAMPUS ENVIRONMENT

Regular communication among minority staff, the black/faculty staff caucus, and leaders of other campus ethnic groups help keep the chancellor and the entire university community attuned to important minority issues. Frequent meetings encourage cooperation through continual involvement of minority staff and help provide a supportive working environment.

With the support of the black caucus of the state legislature, UMass/Boston created an Institute for the Study of Black Culture. The Institute is named after William Monroe Trotter, the Boston-born militant founder of the *Guardian* and the National Equal Rights League. Various campus agencies sponsor minority speakers, and, with the approval of the board of trustees, UMass regularly awards honorary degrees to black leaders. The campus regularly recognizes outstanding leaders in Boston's black community.

OUTCOMES

Several measures provide quantitative indicators of UMass/Boston's success in achieving significant minority presence in the university. During a period a renewed overall growth in undergraduate enrollment, minority enrollment increased even more and now stands at 18 percent of all matriculated undergraduates. The most recently available study (1984) shows that UMass/Boston enrolls 40 percent of the black students who attend public four-year colleges and universities in Massachusetts. The full-time faculty is 13 percent minority; the professional staff 22 percent, and the classified staff 23 percent. But these numbers are important not simply because they are relatively high. Perhaps even more heartening, they reflect a qualitative accomplishment: they exemplify a campus climate in which minorities feel assured of the opportunity to persist and succeed.

Of course, the road has not been trouble-free. The Affirmative Action Office is sometimes seen as impeding the normal search process. And that, indeed, is one of its functions, for the "normal" search process may or may not yield results in hiring women and minority candidates. Change inevitably engenders some resistance. Faculty and staff members sometimes still refer to women or minority candidates as "affirmative action candidates," thus implying that they would be appointed because of procedural requirements, not individual merit.

Further, retention and graduation of minority students must be improved. Data show that minority students persist as well as white students during the first semester of attendance at UMass/Boston. However, retention of some minority groups, blacks in particular, falls off more rapidly in later semesters, and proportionately fewer minority students graduate than white students. UMass is working to find out why minority students are leaving in later semesters, and to create a plan of action to prevent it.

LESSONS FROM THE UMASS/BOSTON EXPERIENCE

- *Leadership from the top is vital.* If minority presence is to be an institutional value, then it must be one of the very limited number of issues (surely not more than two or three) that the chief executive officer chooses for his/her own personal focus of energy and intellect, both on the campus and in the community.

- *External leadership should complement internal activity.* College and university presidents are respected and potentially powerful civic leaders. The commitment of senior administrators to minority participation in the university is greatly strengthened when it is part of a consistent and visible effort to increase minority participation in business and government.

■ *Creating a pluralistic campus requires extra energy and extra money.* Continual renewal of commitment is hard, but essential. Furthermore, a substantial presence of minorities on campus is critical to an institutional climate in which all feel valued, supported, and energized.

■ *Nontraditional measures must be incorporated in admissions evaluation.* National data indicate that minority people tend to have lower SAT scores and class standings than white students. UMass/Boston has good academic support and skills-building programs, and data show that SAT scores are not predictors of grade point average at the university.

UMass/Boston's sense of self changed through concerted effort at all levels, but particularly through leadership. The Boston community's sense of the university has also changed. Substantially free from the racial violence that scarred the city, UMass/Boston has seen itself, and been seen as, a leader in the creation of an environment in which minority participation is valued and sought.

Miami-Dade Community College

A ny community college mindful of its name must be inextricably bound to the community it serves. Miami-Dade Community College (M-DCC) reflects this commitment to the surrounding community in practice and philosophy. In addition to the
normal array of college programs and activities, M-DCC trains all
county police officers and fire fighters, and sponsors Citizens
Against Crime and a book fair that annually brings tens of thousands
of residents and tourists into the streets of what had been considered
the "blighted downtown" area. In addition, the college has provided
instruction in English and employability skills to over 8,000 refugees.
Each year it contributes 25,000 people to the community with one to
three years of education beyond high school, resulting in an estimated productivity increase of $60,000,000.

BACKGROUND AND SETTING

To understand M-DCC and the community it serves, a short-term
historical perspective is critical. M-DCC first opened in 1960 to an
all-white, overwhelmingly non-Hispanic student body of approximately 2,000. Integration came the following year. Twenty-eight
years later, the college serves over 65,000 persons; more than two-
thirds of whom are minority. Fifty percent are Hispanic and 16 percent are Black. Miami-Dade leads the nation in number
of Hispanic and foreign students, and is fourth in number of black
students.

Miami is a city with no majority. It is characterized by extreme diversity and newness. So new is its mix of people that over 79 percent
were born outside of Florida or the U.S. Currently one out of every
11 is a refugee who arrived in the 1980s. The accompanying tran-
sience brings its own set of problems. The area leads the nation in
crime, much of it drug-related, and the state is among the bottom ten
in retaining students until high school graduation.

Miami's greatest potential strength as well as its greatest potential
weakness lies in its diversity. A strong educational system can help
unify the residents of an area, develop individuals' skills that will enhance their self-worth and enable them to make greater contributions, and ultimately improve society. In order for Miami-Dade to
succeed in its mission, it has striven to serve as a model of an institu-

tion built upon, valuing, and able to develop diverse talents. At the same time it has sought to meet the unique and changing needs of its community.

COMMITMENT TO QUALITY AND DIVERSITY

The commitment to provide quality education for minorities must be constantly reaffirmed at all levels of an institution. Similarly, each program and service plays a role in enhancing diversity. Active participation by all is necessary to make a commitment to quality and diversity which are central to the mission of the college. Those in top leadership positions, however, must establish a climate that will support the specific activities that translate commitment into results.

The First Phase

In 1975, Miami-Dade began a three-year study of its general education requirements. As the study progressed, it became clear that the critical issue was the declining academic skills of entering students, and that the institution's educational program would require fundamental change. The goal of the systematic reform was to permit continuation of the open door and at the same time strengthen standards and increase the educational achievement of graduates. The resulting program is more direct and has far greater controls than existed previously. It raises performance expectations and provides increased feedback and assistance to students. Essentially M-DCC rewrote its "open door" policy to provide continued access, but with excellence.

Although that initial reform process is complete in the sense that goals and objectives have been achieved, an evolutionary process is never "done." The original, intensive scrutiny of student support systems revealed weaknesses in other aspects of service delivery. It was clear that culturally diverse students bring their backgrounds, experiences, and preferences with them to the classroom and instructors must understand their effect and impact on the educational process. Attention needed to be focused on the very heart of the college's operation: the teaching/learning relationship.

The Second Phase

In 1986, Miami-Dade initiated the comprehensive, multiyear Teaching/Learning Project, the second major reform. First, a process of consensus building was initiated that culminated in the official adoption of seven institutional values related to teaching and learning; three of these specifically reaffirm the college's commitment to diversity. Perhaps more important, over 3,000 faculty, administrators, staff, and students agreed to key indicators through which M-DCC demonstrates these values. President Robert McCabe strengthened the initiative by announcing that he would evaluate his management team on criteria derived from these indicators. Even more boldly, he asked the board of trustees to hold him similarly accountable.

Institutional policies related to evaluation and the reward system especially must be congruent with institutional values. Individuals must be encouraged and supported to develop essential expertise, and those with skills and interests in critical need areas should be encouraged to assume leadership roles. Positive efforts must be appropriately rewarded and meaningful distinctions must be made between individuals performing differently. Aligning M-DCC's evaluation and reward systems with its stated values concerning service to a diverse student body is a key objective of the Teaching/Learning Project. This move has been applauded by faculty and staff and, when achieved, will further enhance the climate for serving a multiethnic student body.

PROGRAMS TO ENHANCE STUDENT DIVERSITY

Miami-Dade Community College, through its four campuses and many outreach centers, offers more than 100 programs and activities designed to assist minority student and enhance diversity. The following have been selected as a representative sample of the many existing efforts.

Reach-out (recruitment)

The College Reach-Out Program matches grant funds from the state with M-DCC Foundation dollars. While each campus develops programs specific to its feeder area needs, the broad goals of the program are the same: to provide minority and disadvantaged high school and junior high school students information about postsecondary education; to lower barriers that frequently decrease minority participation in postsecondary education (academic preparation, tuition costs); to increase motivation to continue beyond high school. School counselors are key players in the Reach-Out effort; each year M-DCC offers information and strategies and provides programs to help counselors encourage promising students to continue their education. Students who remain with the program for four years receive college scholarships.

Program components are often geared toward the special interest of students in the target groups. For example, an ambitious fine arts festival couples the creative efforts of feeder high school drama departments and M-DCC faculty and staff. Participating students experience one aspect of college life in which they already demonstrate skill and interest, in a manner designed to leave them with positive feelings and a sense of their own enhanced competence. In addition, day-long programs are planned that bring Reach-Out students to a campus to deal with specific issues. A summer program that provides a combination of college courses and work in a public hospital is another option available to minority high school graduates interested in health-care careers.

In 1987-88, through the college-wide array of programs, Reach-Out touched approximately 6,000 students and 300 to 400 parents and teachers. Plans are currently underway to track participating students.

Black Student Opportunity Program (recruitment/retention)

This new county-wide program represents activist response to the disturbing decline in black student enrollment in higher education over the past ten years. The major objectives of the Black Student Opportunity Program are: to motivate a significant number of black high school students to enroll in college preparatory courses and to reach for a higher level of achievement; to increase the number of well-prepared black high school graduates who aspire to a college education; to help students achieve a high school diploma, pursue an associate degree at M-DCC, and then transfer to a university; and to provide necessary financial aid to participating students.

Through three years of high school, selected students are exposed to basic skills testing; prescriptive course selection; test-taking skill development; enhancement of critical thinking skills; career planning programs; and summer work internships. Participants are paired with mentors carefully chosen from the business community. Similar support will be provided as they continue their careers at M-DCC.

A unique feature of the Black Student Opportunity Program is the component that addresses financing postsecondary study. While in high school, each student is rewarded for performance in designated college preparatory courses. Funds provided by community sponsors

will accumulate into a "bank account" established in the name of
each student and will be matched by the M-DCC Foundation. The
monies may be spent on M-DCC tuition (with the payment plan continuing) as well as on tuition for the upper-division college of the student's choice.

A similar program is currently being planned to assist Hispanic
students.

Comprehensive Opportunity to Pursue Excellence (retention)

During the mid-1980s, a small group of faculty and administrative
staff became concerned about the significant number of students
who were dropping out of their courses before the end of each semester. This adhoc group ultimately created the Comprehensive Opportunity to Pursue Excellence (COPE) program to address the problem.
They explored the reasons for student attrition, noting a general inability to deal with the rigors of college. Absence of clear career goals,
family hardships, and a lack of real involvement within the college
environment were common problems identified. COPE began to
match these high-risk students, mostly minorities, with trained faculty and staff "facilitators." Most semesters, close to 200 students per
semester are so matched. Facilitators meet informally with the students on a regular basis, working with them to resolve the issues,
many external to the classroom, that often interfere with academic
success.

COPE efforts continue to expand and now include tutoring, counseling, a summer institute, and the Jump Start program, which is designed for high school graduates who are ambivalent about plans for
higher education. It allows them to attend college classes and receive
special support services for six weeks during the summer term. Thus,
they may "sample" college experience in a smaller, more personal-
ized setting. After the program conducted in the summer, 71 percent
of Jump Start participants enrolled at M-DCC for the following fall
term. Even more rewarding is this statistical comparison: the national average retention rate at two-year public institutions is 52 percent, while the retention rate of high-risk students in the COPE
program is 82 percent.

Challenge Center (retention)

The Challenge Center provides an integrated academic and student
support network to approximately 180 participating black students

each year. Individuals are referred to the Challenge Center if they are newly enrolled full-time students with marginal basic skills assessment test results. The program is particularly geared to assist students who, by profile, would appear to benefit from support as they enter the regular academic mainstream. Individuals clearly requiring remedial assistance are referred to other programs.

Challenge Center services include a tutorial laboratory, a mentoring program, a student development course focusing on the enhancement of self-management skills, and a course leading toward the clarification of career goals. Through a series of planned social activities, the Challenge Center also assists students in developing their communication skills; provides opportunity for cooperative interchange with peers and authority figures; and facilitates involvement in campus organizations and immersion in college life. The Challenge Center has demonstrated its success with high-risk students. The average GPA after a year of academic work is 2.5; 75 percent of participants re-enroll from one academic year to the next.

Urban Community College Transfer Opportunity Program (facilitating minority transfer)

Barriers to minority success in postsecondary education were identified in a recent three-year project funded by the Ford Foundation. The findings of the project will help improve the assistance Miami-Dade provides to minority students who plan to transfer to upper-division institutions. Minority students who feel excluded from the mainstream of college or university life often fail to form the supportive networks with peers, faculty, and student organizations that can make the difference between perseverance and attrition. The bewildering institutional processes of registration, application for financial aid, and finding housing, coupled with academic demands may be overwhelming. Resulting from this project will be a model for successful transition for minority students, including retention strategies, "survival skills," and strengthened articulation with the college's principal feeder universities.

PROGRAMS TO ENHANCE EMPLOYEE AWARENESS AND DIVERSITY

An institution demonstrates commitment to serve a multiethnic population in ways that go beyond programming. Employees need opportunity to enhance their knowledge and refine their skills in interacting with the diverse student body. This becomes especially critical for faculty who interact directly with students in the learning environment. There must also be recognition that diversity must be reflected in the composition of the faculty and staff. Demonstrating commitment to this belief, in 1987, with full approval of the board of trustees, President McCabe mandated that 50 percent of all new faculty and professional staff hires be minority.

Faculty Recruitment

The average Miami-Dade Community College faculty member has been at the college more than 15 years. Thus, it is not surprising that they are overwhelmingly non-Hispanic white. In order to have a pool of qualified minority applicants as positions become available, a minority vita bank has been established. Recruitment efforts are channeled through this program and open positions are advertised in publications with large minority readership. Comprehensive listings of minority professional and civic organizations have been compiled and a network established with graduate schools to help develop an interest in faculty positions with Miami-Dade.

Administrative Internships

Beginning in 1989, administrative internships will be offered to interested minority faculty and professional staff within M-DCC. While still in the planning stage, the program objective is clear: to assist minority faculty and staff in developing skills needed to succeed in administrative positions at the college. The program will be particularly helpful to the number of minority personnel hired in recent years who tend to be clustered at lower levels of the organizational ladder. A real commitment to minority success demands more than simply placing individuals into new roles—it also means providing the tools that will allow them to succeed in those positions.

Graduate Course

A graduate course developed jointly by M-DCC teaching faculty and faculty from the University of Miami School of Education is scheduled to be implemented in January 1989. Entitled "Teaching and Learning in Higher Education," much of the course is devoted to cultural factors that affect learning styles and preferences, and their implications for the instructor and his/her repertoire of teaching strategies. All faculty new to M-DCC will be required to take this course prior to receiving tenure, and experienced faculty will be encouraged to take it.

Staff Development

Across the district and on each campus, staff development funds are allocated annually; approximately 25 percent of the funds are earmarked for minority affairs. Numerous activities are planned to heighten staff awareness and to identify strategies that support minority student needs. Recently, topics have included cross-cultural communication, retention of black athletes, developing third-world awareness in social science courses, and cultural influences on learning styles.

External consultants frequently meet with faculty or administrative planning groups to provide needed expertise to help assess ongoing efforts, or to assist in the development of new programming. Consultants have been retained by the college to develop strategies to improve minority recruitment efforts; to promote communication patterns among M-DCC personnel that will enhance interethnic understanding; and to expand teaching alternatives that will enhance the learning potential of minority students and non-native speakers of English.

SUMMARY

Even with a supportive climate and with clear commitment from the highest levels of the college's administration, the challenge of enhancing diversity is not simple. If anything has been learned over the past 20 years, the following "truths" have emerged from evaluating what has worked and what has not:

1. There is no more homogeneity within any group known as "minority" than there is in the "majority." To be truly sensitive and responsive to needs, schools must recognize and address many distinct factors.

2. Similarly, "service" cannot be simply and easily developed; neither can it be generally defined. The entire institution must respond with attention to specific needs.

3. Because diversity demands different kinds of service, it is important to set clear objectives and assess progress toward them. There is a constant danger of stretching resources too far to support the level of programming needed for success.

4. Those programs that seem to work best, as defined by student success, have active participation in their design and administration by individuals who are closest and most committed to its goals.

Additionally, those most affected by the outcomes (students) must have significant input.

Accommodating minorities on campus inevitably requires substantial financial investment and results in a drain on other resources. It taxes people's ingenuity, energy, and commitment. So why bother? If the M-DCC experience of a 20-year, ongoing attempt to enhance and celebrate diversity is illustrative, an institution "bothers" because the payoffs are so great: growth for students, faculty, and staff; enrichment of the educational experience far beyond what any formal curriculum might deliver; the satisfaction that comes from providing access to education to all interested individuals and thus the potential to share in the good things this society has to offer. The rewards for Miami-Dade Community College and for the people of Miami have been considerable. The M-DCC community believes that the investment has been a sound one for all.

Mount St. Mary's College Strides Toward Educational Proficiency (S.T.E.P.) Program

"Before I went to the summer workshop at the Doheny Campus of Mount St. Mary's, I wasn't even thinking of going to college. Now, I know I need to go. I have to go. Hearing the goals of college freshmen made me realize I can't do anything if I stop school after high school."

BACKGROUND

Mount St. Mary's College, a Catholic liberal arts college primarily for women, opened its main campus 63 years ago in the Santa Monica Hills of West Los Angeles. A strong arts and science curriculum undergirded the baccalaureate degree program. Nursing and education programs were added in response to community needs.

In 1960, when community colleges were becoming more prevalent in California, Mount St. Mary's opened a two-year program on its second campus as an alternative for students who wanted a value-based education and who had the potential for college but who were not academically prepared to enter the four-year program. Since the opening of the Doheny campus, significant numbers of students have successfully completed the associate degree program and transferred to the Mount's baccalaureate program or to other four-year colleges.

STUDENT PROFILE

The 1986 Doheny campus freshman class reflected the cultural diversity of the Southern California area: 56.7 percent Hispanic, 18 percent black and 9.8 percent Asian. In addition, 98 percent of the class were first-generation college students. Over half came from families living at or below the poverty level. For the most part, these students embody all the characteristics of the typical high-risk student: their high school grade point average (GPA) is between 1.7 and 2.5; their SAT scores average 658 (often reflecting poor language preparation and learning skills); they come from low socioeconomic background; they are the first in their families to attend college; most work off campus; and many are commuters. These students have no models who successfully completed college; often, few in their family or neighborhood have graduated from high school. Many of their families are uninformed about the demands made on a college student, and understandably reluctant to lose their income and unpaid services. Many students have had poor preparation in high school, or are immigrants with language difficulties.

STRATEGIES

Mount St. Mary's helps these students succeed in college by providing a supportive environment, with individual attention, intervention when difficulties appear, and close communication with faculty and administration.

Admissions and Testing

The program for disadvantaged students begins with admissions. Students who have a GPA of 2.0 or higher are admitted; those with a GPA below 2.0 are interviewed, and their potential for success in college is assessed. If they show promise, are motivated, and wish to attend college, they are accepted. Once accepted into the associate program, all students are tested. They select a tentative schedule of skills courses (reading development, basic math, composition, and study skills) and regular college courses, with the help of an advisor.

Required Skills Classes

Students are required to take remedial classes in areas where testing shows they are weak. These classes are graded "credit"/"no credit" so that a student can repeat courses until she reaches the required level of competence without affecting her GPA. Students are encouraged to get a head start on college by taking some skills courses in the Summer Skills Program. This is a free, voluntary, intensive three-week program that offers reading, math, writing, and review of scientific thinking. Students choose two of these based on their advisors' recommendations, and all take a required course in study skills. Personal assessment and individual advisement by college faculty and staff are the key to making this first experience a success.

Extended Orientation

Students must take a semester-long orientation course. Here, they meet weekly with a small group of their peers and a faculty/staff mentor to discuss concerns and difficulties. The group helps students to solve problems and to look at their own gifts, abilities, and goals in a positive and realistic manner. During the course of the semester, each student does a personal gifts assessment, a personal skills inventory and a career exploration project, which she discusses with the director of the Career Center.

Learning Resource Center

In conjunction with the Freshman English course, each student must spend one additional hour per week at the Learning Resource Center, where she works with a tutor on an individualized plan designed by her English instructor. Tutors in this center are adults who have had experience as elementary school teachers, and who are warm and caring individuals. Students are also encouraged to take advantage of individualized instructional computer software in reading, English composition, and basic mathematics. Frequently, instructors design learning packages so the student, working at her own pace, can use them to reinforce classroom learning. The instructor and the tutor communicate regularly regarding the student's progress.

Early Warning System

Instructors notify the student and her advisor early in the semester (October and March) of any difficulties the student may be having in a course. The advisor meets with the students to determine the cause of the difficulty and to suggest a course of action. The dean consults with the advisor and then sees each student who receives two or more of these early warning notices, reinforcing the necessity of taking the corrective action recommended by the advisor. Student, advisor, and dean meet again at mid-semester, if the student is in danger of receiving a grade lower than a "C." Those achieving less than a 2.0 semester GPA are placed on academic probation for the next semester. A support group, facilitated by a trained counselor, meets to assist these students, and most are back in good standing by the next semester.

Residence

In the last four years, the housing capacity of the Doheny campus has increased from 35 to 170 beds. The college encourages students to live on campus and funds many of them. The residence program is designed to support and assist the students to mature and to develop a sense of responsibility. For many students, residence is the only way to insure a quiet, orderly place and uninterrupted time to study. Commuter students can also be successful, with faculty and staff going out of their way to help non-residents cope with the additional challenges they face: time management, transportation needs, and family responsibilities.

Courses in the Baccalaureate Program

Students are encouraged to take courses in areas of strength and, in their second year, to take at least one course in the baccalaureate program. This allows the student to make the utmost of her potential and to move as quickly as possible into her chosen major. Many of the Asian students, for example, are strong in mathematics and science, but weak in communication skills. These students may take math or science courses in the baccalaureate program on the main campus and communication skills in the associate program at the Doheny campus. This provides an easy transition to the baccalaureate major. The college provides scheduled shuttle bus service between the two campuses.

Baccalaureate faculty and students meet with associate students to discuss majors, requirements, career options, and careers that Mount St. Mary's College alumnae have pursued. Counselors from the California state system also visit the Doheny campus, holding information sessions regarding their baccalaureate programs and meeting individually with interested students.

Career Counseling and Internships

In addition to the career inventory, which is part of extended orientation, the Career Center provides workshops and classes in career exploration, resume writing, and interview techniques. Internships that give academic credit—and sometimes stipends—are available, and students are encouraged to pursue these in their sophomore year. Helping students set realistic career goals and providing concrete and tangible steps that they can accomplish in a relatively short time are important to motivate students from low socioeconomic backgrounds. Thus, many students have an associate degree as a first career goal. When they see that they can earn the A.A., many move on to a higher goal.

Outreach to the Community

Students perform supervised volunteer service in community agencies, and share these experiences in seminars conducted by faculty members as part of the outreach component of the associate program. The group works at deriving meaning from each student's outreach experiences, relating them to academic learning and larger social issues. The student keeps a journal of her experience, and the agency supervisor submits a written evaluation. Speakers and films are also a part of the seminars, and these introduce the student to various social problems connected with her volunteer work. Students realize they can contribute positively to society, clarify their career goals, and become more aware of social problems. Many students are motivated to continue as volunteers.

English as a Second Language Program

Students of ability who are not fluent in English, perhaps because they are recent immigrants to the United States, can enroll in the Mount's English as a Second Language program concurrently with their communications skills classes. The foreign language approach often makes the difference between success and failure for non-native speakers enrolled in the associate program.

Cultural Awareness

Administrators and faculty in the associate program have long been aware that cultural values and expectations influence how a student learns. A recent Consortium for the Advancement of Private Higher Education (CAPHE) grant has enabled members of the college faculty and staff to develop multicultural tools to help students, both in the classroom and support services. One project, for example, is a bibliography of literature by black, Hispanic, and Asian women for use in English classes. Students of all ethnic backgrounds find respect for their heritage in the associate program, which helps them to feel more at home in the college environment. The predominantly Anglo faculty is trained in understanding the educational significance of cultural diversity through a series of workshops. Workshops include topics such as the academic background of minority students and how to build on the strengths of different cultures. Support is provided to each department to study minority issues or resources. Results are disseminated through workshops and campus newsletters.

OUTCOMES

A high proportion of students—65 to 70 percent of those who enter as freshmen—complete the Associate in Arts degree. In 1986, 86 percent of the freshman class completed the first year; 71 percent returned for the second year or transferred into the baccalaureate program. Most of those not returning transferred to other baccalaureate programs. The retention rate for Hispanics is extremely high, with 95 percent of the Hispanics in that class returning for a second semester or transferring into the baccalaureate program. Mount St. Mary's attributes this success to the coordinated program of academic development and support services outlined above.

Graduates of the S.T.E.P. program continue to perform well in their upper-division study; their GPAs decline only .01 percent. Further, 50 percent of students completing their associate degree receive their bachelor's degree from MSMC, and 20 to 30 percent do so at other four-year colleges. Some are now in masters and Ph.D programs.

INSTITUTIONAL IMPLICATIONS

Although there has been a consistency of purpose, and the assumptions underlying the initiation and development of the program have remained constant, controversy has not been absent. Significant institutional commitment is required: (1) to support the development and implementation of academic and student life support systems; (2) to sustain the heavy financial aid programs; and (3) to deal with faculty reluctance to cope with the wide difference in preparation among the freshmen on the two campuses. The Associate in Arts staff, which meets bi-monthly, has struggled with such questions as: should all students be tested? should skill classes be required? should high-risk students be admitted? should extended probation be granted? what should be the content and extent of orientation? what are the most effective teaching methodologies? how can learning be made more active? what are appropriate student services? how can residence programs be made more effective? what are effective assessment techniques?

FUTURE DIRECTIONS

Assessing and monitoring the program continues. Each year the program is adjusted to reflect the evaluations of students, faculty, and staff. Areas still needing improvement include increased utilization by faculty of active learning techniques, and increased developmental programs for resident students and those in the student service area. Students seem to be more successful in courses where collaborative learning projects and cooperative study groups are encouraged by the faculty. Resident programs need to be linked more integrally to the academic and skills areas. Plans call for student services to sponsor activities designed around the developmental needs of students. A study is in process to assess the strengths and impact of the various components of the program; its results will determine future directions.

Program administrators at Mount St. Mary's College believe that one of the major advantages of undertaking such a program in an independent college is its ability to be responsive to need and change. The program remains consistent in its assumptions and basic programmatic development, while being dynamic and vital in responding to the current needs of students.

Endnote

This *Handbook* has tried to capture and report the many different initiatives that colleges and universities have taken to make American higher education pluralistic and diverse, to reflect the richness of our society and the potential of all its citizens.

It is hardly the final word. Indeed, we are painfully aware that the current conceptual framework is not fully adequate; in some areas, we need new language to shape the discussion. The Board of Directors of the American Council on Education intended this document to represent a beginning—a beginning of renewed commitment, a point of departure for new approaches for the development of new paradigms and new insights. If historians and educators look at this book 20 or 25 years from now, we hope that they will find it a curiously dated reminder of how higher education has changed, and how much progress has been made in conceptualizing the issues, framing the language of discussion, and designing strategies for positive change.

If this effort and the many others underway nationally are successful, future discussions of pluralism on campus will be much more sophisticated; many of the suggestions in this book will be so commonplace there would be no reason to single them out.

We have tried in the *Handbook* to capture the state of the art, knowing how primitive that state is. If it succeeds in any measure in revitalizing the dialogue on minority participation, in advancing our knowledge and understanding, it will have been a success.